DATE DUE

OC 5 '08			
OC - 2 '09			

DEMCO 38-296

The Wind and the Waves
Four Modern Korean Poets

The Wind and the Waves
Four Modern Korean Poets

Translated and Introduced by
Sung-Il Lee

ASIAN HUMANITIES PRESS
Berkeley, California

' Paperbacks

s offer to the specialist
ν translations of major
works and significant original contributions, to enhance our understanding of Asian religions, cultures and thought.

"Asian Humanities Press" and "AHP Paperbacks" are trademarks of Jain Publishing Company.

ISBN 0-89581-917-1
Library of Congress Catalog Card Number 88-83534

Printed in the United States of America

Library of Congress Cataloging in Publication Data:
The Wind and the waves: four modern Korean poets / translated and
  introduced by Sung-Il Lee.
      p.   cm.
    ISBN 0-89581-917-1: $12.00
    1. Korean poetry—20th century—Translations into English.
  2. English poetry—20th century—Translations from Korean. I. Lee,
  Sung-Il, 1943-
  PL984.E3W56 1989
  895.7'1408—dc20

88-83534
CIP

TO THE MEMORY OF

My Father,

Professor Lee Insoo
(1916-1950)

Contents

Yu Chi-Whan (1908-1967)

Cho Ji-Hoon (1920-1968)

Appendix: Ten Additional Poems Translated by Lee Insoo

Preface

The four poets whose works are presented here in translation are all important figures in twentieth-century Korean literature. Literary taste can vary; and diversity of literary taste often leads to different opinions about the relative merits and demerits of writers. But the unchallenged stature of the four poets has never been questioned by Korean literati. Indeed, the poetic spirit each of them embraced was of the highest kind; and one might say that the Miltonic equation of *poeta* and *poema* is true to the fact as far as these poets are concerned.

By limiting the scope of this anthology to the works of the four writers, however, I am not implying that they are the only noteworthy poets of twentieth-century Korea. What has impelled me to this task is the spiritual affinity that binds them together, although each poet's works reveal his unique world-view and literary temper. My personal reverence for them, not only as writers but as men of integrity, has also made me envision a book of this kind.

A number of poems appearing in this volume may already have been translated by others. But my belief is that a poem is a living entity—it has its own life, which no translated version can augment or alter. It can and should ask for as many renditions as possible until the most approximate to the poet's real voice is heard. Despite my knowledge that a translator is after all a traitor—to the original works and to the poets who wrote them—, I have worked, as any translator would, cherishing the hope that somehow I may do justice to the original poems.

The ultimate goal of a translator of poetry is to make felt in the translated version the correspondence between sound and sense achieved in the original work. The task involves transplanting not only the sense but the sound of a poem written in the vernacular into another linguistic soil. Literal translation, if there is any such, is bound to fail in attaining this goal, for the two languages involved—such as Korean and English—have completely different linguistic characteristics and cultural backgrounds. For a translated version to be successful, it must contain the same overall sound effect, such as rhythm and the flow of verses, as well as the same message, as the original. Translation is not simply a matter of changing the garb of language; it is the process of making a poem reborn as its equivalent in another language. All this, of course, is more easily said than done. And if the reader finds any flaws in versification in this volume, I am solely responsible for them.

Most of the work was done during my sojourn at the University of Toronto, where I was a visiting professor of Korean literature in 1987. While I was working on this book, Professor Frank Watt and Professor R. Morton Smith, both published poets, kindly read my manuscripts and gave me invaluable suggestions. Professor Chai-Shin Yu in the Department of East Asian Studies made my sojourn at Toronto a meaningful one with his kind interest in my work and the friendship he bestowed on me. I thank Mr. M. Jain, President of the Asian Humanities Press, and Professor Lewis Lancaster at the University of California at Berkeley, Editor of the Press, for their decision to publish this work. I am deeply indebted to the Korean Culture and Arts Foundation for providing a subsidy to defray the cost of the printing. Throughout the period when I was absorbed in this work, my wife Cremilda remained a careful reader, and her perceptive comments often made me go back to the original poems to recast my translations.

My deepest gratitude is due to my long-deceased father, Professor Lee Insoo, whose own translations of Korean poetry have shown me how to approach the task. I have not attempted to translate the works already translated by him. But the poems he translated decades ago are among the best works of the four poets, and should not be omitted from an anthology of their poetry. For this reason, I have provided an appendix containing ten poems translated by my father. This slim volume, though an inadequate one, I dedicate to his memory.

Seoul
January, 1989

Introduction

The four poets, whose works appear in translation in this volume, all lived through the most turbulent times in modern Korean history. Yi Yook-Sa (1904-1944) lived and died while Korea remained a nation deprived of her sovereignty. His lifetime almost coincided with the period when Korea was under the forceful rule of Japan, which lasted for more than three decades. Yoon Dong-Ju (1917-1945) also had to spend all his lifetime during the Japanese occupation of Korea. Both Yi Yook-Sa and Yoon Dong-Ju died before the country regained her national sovereignty. Thus the two poets lived during the darkest period of the nation's history. Yu Chi-Whan (1908-1967) and Cho Ji-Hoon (1920-1968) also spent their youthful years during the Japanese reign, but they lived to see the end of the Second World War, which brought along the nation's liberation. During their lifetime, they had to witness yet another national tragedy, the Korean War, which broke out in 1950 and devastated the country for the next few years. The end of the war, however, was not the end of the nation's suffering. Two major political events, the Students' Uprising in 1960, which toppled the first regime established after the nation's liberation, and the military *coup* of 1961, which has left a far-reaching impact on the political conditions in Korea, both occurred during their lifetime. When Yu Chi-Whan and Cho Ji-Hoon died, Korea was still groping for political and economic stability, which then seemed so far away.

One might suspect that a poet's inner life is not to be affected much by the external conditions, for it is a solitary probing into the meaning of his existence. The world of introspection may be considered alien to the external affairs that happen around him. But a poet is also a social being; and his inner life is affected by his encounter with the external world. What a poet writes is often an outcome of the encounter between his world of introspection and the world in which he leads his physical life. A poet rejoices in life but he also suffers; and the private suffering he undergoes as an introspective man becomes intensified by the general human conditions he witnesses.

The above generalization, however, is not made with a view to asserting that the works written by the four poets have their significance only as products of the age in which they lived. Regardless of the socio-political conditions that must have affected their spiritual lives, they retained, as any poet should, their own worlds of introspection that transcend the bounds of their age and, therefore, have permanent values. Their poetic spirits, that would have flowered in whatever socio-political conditions, found their outlets within the conditions of their age and gave birth to the poems that appear in this volume. We must not read these poems simply as a reflection of the age or as an outcome of the introspective men's effort to come to terms with the times they lived in. We should rather look at them as manifestations of their struggle to assert the meaning of life with the voices allowed only to those who can transcend the yoke of time and place with their all-seeing eyes.

Yi Yook-Sa (1904-1944) was a descendant of Yi Hwang, the foremost Confucian scholar-philosopher of the Yi Dynasty, the last monarchy in Korea. He grew up receiving strict moral discipline from his grandfather, who taught him classical Chinese from his childhood. His grandfather on his mother's side was also a man of learning, who raised an army to fight the invading Japanese toward the end of the dynasty. Born in such a distinguished family, Yi Yook-Sa led a life worthy of his lineage. He spent all his life for the cause of national sovereignty, and died in prison. His involvement in political activities started in his early twenties. When he was twenty-one, he organized with two of his brothers a secret society named "Ui-yol-tan," a gathering of patriotic youths. He went to Peking, when he was twenty-three, to promote liaison between his own underground organization and those who were engaged in the same activity in China. The next year he was arrested by the Japanese police for having been involved in the bombing of a bank—which, as were all the other banks in Korea then, was a channel of economic exploitation of Korea by the Japanese—and stayed in prison for a couple of years. His prison cell number was *264;* and later, he adopted "Yook-Sa" as his pen name,* after the Korean pronunciation of 6 and 4—2 being pronounced the same as his family name Yi in Korean. "Yook-Sa," as he transcribed it in Chinese letters, means "the history of the

---

*His real name was Yi Won-Rock.

continent." From then on, the rest of his life was filled with repeated arrests and imprisonments. When he was twenty-nine, he enrolled in a military academy Koreans had built in Peking with a view to training future military leaders. A member of the first graduating class of the academy, he was arrested a number of times on various occasions. Finally, he was sent to a prison in Peking, then under Japanese occupation. There he died from torture. He was forty.

Indeed, one wonders how he could possibly write poems at all while spending most of his lifetime as a political activist. He did not write many poems—only thirty-six, including three written in Chinese. He started writing poems when he was already thirty; thus, all of his poems were written during the last ten years of his life, the period when he was most actively engaged in political activities. Writing poetry requires free time and leisure, and with our knowledge of Yi Yook-Sa's life, we cannot but wonder at his poetic achievement. But the very fact that he lived such an intense life reversely explains how he could write those poems, which, though not many in number, reveal a poetic spirit and refinement in technique that belong to the highest order. In considering his poetry we must exclude the notion that poems can be written only in leisure, for his poetry was a summation of his inner life that compelled him to do what he did as a public man. His poetry was an intense expression of his passion for his native land, beauty and truth, and life itself.

The innumerable essays he wrote attest the intellectual vigor that drove him to studying diverse subjects. He wrote on metaphysics, natural sciences, international politics, socio-political problems in Asia, social and cultural history of Korea, and modern Chinese history. But most of all, he was a leading literary critic in his days. He was a man of exceptional mind and knowledge. Neither the image of a poet encaged in his private world nor the image of a man of action alien to the moments of introspection or intellectual probing will do as a truthful picture of Yi Yook-Sa. Indeed, he was both—a man passionately dedicated to political activities for the patriotic cause, and a man no less passionately absorbed in the world of introspection and the realm of intellect. In Yi Yook-Sa we see what Yeats called 'the unity of being.' His poetry is a manifestation of the fusion of the contrasting elements in life that appear mutually exclusive—the soul and the body, passion and reason, intellect and action, and, most of all, the world of poetry and the world of politics. By saying so, however, I do not mean that, for Yi Yook-Sa, poetry was a vehicle for his political thoughts. On the contrary, poetry often provided him with moments of temporary relief from the pressing thoughts of politics, from which he was never free at any moment in his life. Thus, we meet in his poetry a man who had a seething passion for his country and political ideology but could become pensive and even dreamy at moments of introspection.

The dual aspects of his poetry thus create a kind of rhythm—alternation of austere moral and indulgence in the world of sensuality, of patriotic zeal and the poise and calm attained in pensive mood, of grief and anger for his country's fate and affirmation of life as a whole. Watching the misery of his nation, he compares it to that of a bat deprived of the bliss of living in the light ('Bat'); he envisages his homeland as a place where only "graves lie moss-grown, with no butterflies around" ('A Midnight Song'); and an outburst of grief and anger for the fate of his nation is heard in the surging lines of 'The Sea Waves.' But he asserts the beauty of life, the unvanquishable life-force that persists even in the extreme conditions, and he can even indulge in the reverie of "a castle of flowers" where "memories throng like dreaming butterflies" ('Flowers'). That he was a man full of compassion for all mankind is well expressed in 'Evening Glow' and 'Let us Sing of a Star.' The fact that he was a lifelong fighter does not mean that he was a man of hatred. His concern for the fate of his nation made him a politically-active man, but he was capable of feeling the common bond of humanity. An austere moralist, he was also capable of momentary indulgence in the world of sensuality, in which he saw an undeniable part of human existence:

> The splendor of life dazzling like a rainbow—
> A world worth to live, while sinning. ('Opium')

Indeed, it is a futile attempt to look for political ideology in his poetry. Sheer lyricism untinged with worldly concerns often overflows his lines:

> As the sea bares her bosom to the sky,
> A white-sailed boat will come adrift,
>
> And my longed-for guest will finally arrive
> With his weary limbs draped in green. ('Green Grapes')

Yi Yook-Sa's first literary training was in classical Chinese, and in his poetry we see the influence of the versification in classical Chinese poetry characterized by regularity in rhythm. Most of his poems are made up of stanzas containing the same number of lines; and within each stanza verses develop, maintaining a certain rhythm. In many cases, one can detect a regular beat repeated throughout a stanza:

> In the freezing dawn on an arctic tundra,
> Deep in the snow the sprouts stir,
> Waiting for the legion of swallows—
> A promise not to be broken at last! ('Flowers')

A similar kind of regularity in versification is observable even in the poems written in free verse:

> On the primeval morn,
> When the sky was dawning,
> Somewhere indeed a cock crew loud.
>
> When all the mountains
> Were rushing to the ocean with longing,
> They could not invade this wild plain.
>
> Through endless time
> Seasons bloomed and faded diligently,
> Till a vast stream found its way at last.
>
> Now snow falls
> And plum-blossoms' fragrance fills the air,
> Here I am sowing my scanty seeds of a song.
>
> After an infinite flow of time,
> He who arrives on a white horse
> Shall sing it loudly upon this plain. ('The Wild Plain')

In the above poem each triplet shows a certain pattern in the development of the verses: the first line is short, the second a bit longer, and the third line, being even longer, has a full sweep of breath. What is intended here is the convergence of the message (what is said) and the flow of the verses (how it is uttered). The imaginative scope of the poem is evidenced by the expanse of time covered in it: it encompasses the very beginning of time, the formation of the earth, the present, and an infinite flow of time into the future. The poem is a declaration of Yi Yook-Sa that his poetic spirit will outlast the history of mankind, for it had its origin in the Creation itself. The first crowing of a cock announcing the beginning of the world was the first sound ever heard on this planet; and it was the beginning of the spirit of poesy. After an immeasurable flow of time, finally the poet is "sowing [his] scanty seeds of a song," believing that, after another infinite flow of time, his song will be sung by one "who [will arrive] on a white horse"—one who is no longer human but emblematic of the consecration of his poetic spirit. As the expanse of time is boundless, so is the space envisioned in the poem. That boundless plain is the realm of his poetic spirit, uncontaminated by the doings of mankind —hence the image of the color white: snow, plum-blossoms, a white horse. Here is no spatial notion; and the images drawn from the East and the West are fused together in the poem. The beginning of time is conceived not in terms of the Christian Genesis but the crowing of a cock; the white horse may allude to Pegasus, but white is also the color Koreans cherish most; and the image of plum-blossoms' fragrance filling the air, while snow falls, is typically Korean. The prophetic voice of Yi Yook-Sa declaring the time-defying endurance of his poetic spirit is heard in the lines.

A few of his poems are about the agonizing experience of writing poetry—'My Muse' and 'My Song Flew Away.' Some are self-portraits—'A Monologue' and 'Looking Back.' Both 'A Tall Tree' and 'Lake' may stand as metaphors for the poet himself. But all this classification is meaningless, for the corpus of his poetic writings is a reflection of his whole being as man and poet. In Yi Yook-Sa we see an embodiment of the ideal of the traditional Korean scholar, a man neither enfeebled by the pale cast of thought nor alien to the moments of introspection and pensive mood while remaining a man of action. The convergence of poetic sensibility and intellectual sinew is thus epitomized in the life and poetry of Yi Yook-Sa.

Yoon Dong-Ju (1917-1945) was born in Manchuria, where his parents, as many Koreans did in those days, lived in exile to stay

away from the persecution in the Korean peninsula. His initiation into poetry started early: when he was only twelve, he was already engrossed in writing songs to be printed in what he and his classmates claimed to be their literary journal. After attending a highschool in Manchuria for some time, he transferred to Soong-Shil High School in Pyong-yang, Korea, famed for its nationalist education. But that school was soon closed by the Japanese authorities, because both the teachers and the students there had refused to pay homage to a shrine built to extol the ancestry of the Japanese—a practice forced upon Koreans everywhere in the country then. Yoon Dong-Ju returned to Manchuria, where he graduated from a highschool in 1938. In the same year he entered Yonhi Liberal Arts College in Seoul, which has now become Yonsei University. All these years he had been writing poems, but one can safely assume that most of his better poems were written in his twenties, the last years of his life. After graduating from Yonhi Liberal Arts College in 1941, he went to Japan to study English literature. But his trip to Japan turned out to be a fatal one. He was soon arrested by the police under the suspicion of having been involved in the national independence movement, and died in prison within less than two years of imprisonment. He was twenty-eight. The real cause of his death is not known; but in the letters he wrote in prison to his family he told them that he had been receiving some kind of injection for several months. Most probably, he was being used as an object of 'medical' experiments until he died.*
Those who visited him in prison report that he was losing weight gradually, finally to become like a skeleton.

Yoon Dong-Ju's life was an uneventful one, and one sees in it the quiet growth and the sudden termination of a poetic genius. Even though he died in prison, there is no evidence that he had been engaged in any political activities. He was not a born fighter, as Yi Yook-Sa was. But the very fact that even a passive and introvert young man, whose life consisted only of introspection and inner struggle, had to die as a political prisoner reflects the darkness of the

---

* A Japanese scholar, who has done some research on the cause of Yoon Dong-Ju's death, visited the prison where he died, to look for documents that could explain the cause of his death; but he could not find any, because all documents had been destroyed. Song Mong-Kyu, Yoon Dong-Ju's cousin, who had been imprisoned at that time, also died of the same cause.

age. It does not detract from the stature of Yoon Dong-Ju as a man; it only adds pathos to our reception of his poetry. In some sense, his untimely death was what had been preordained, for while reading his poems we cannot envision him as one who could have become 'a paltry thing, a tattered coat upon a stick.' Yoon Dong-Ju knew it:

> If the cross is to be granted me,
> As it was once to Christ,
> One who suffered gladly,
>
> I shall quietly endure,
> Drooping my head,
> While my blood oozes like flowers
> Beneath the darkening sky. ('The Cross')

He was a sacrificial lamb offered to the altar of poesy, though his persecutors did not know it. Yoon Dong-Ju suffered alone and silently, and he bore the cross for his age, not for the grand cause of national independence but for the consolation that the record of his suffering could provide for youths of later times:

> In a rented room in a foreign land,
> While the night rain whispers outside,
>
> I light a candle to push out the dark,
> And wait for the morn to come like an age.
>
> I offer myself a small hand—
> The first handshake that brings tears and comfort.
>   ('A Poem Easily Written')

The morning he waited for "to come like an age" was the advent of a new era to bring national freedom and hope for the future. It was also the moment of the liberation of his soul, to be achieved through existential awakening. The candle he lights "to push out the dark" —filling not only his room but the world of his consciousness—is his will to attain his ideal self. He sees his present self as a being struggling to fulfill his self. Therefore, as he offers himself "a small hand," emblematic of the promise of the future, he finds consolation in the hope of future self-fulfillment.

Yoon Dong-Ju's poetry reveals that he was a man of conscience. Conscience here means not only probing into one's moral responsibility as a social being. His ethic encompasses both a concern for his role as a social being and a desire to achieve within himself the convergence of his mind and heart, which will make him a complete man. Without sounding like a moralist, therefore, he writes:

> Until I breathe my last breath
> I wish to face my sky without shame.
> Even a wind blowing on leaves
> Has left me restless.
> With a heart singing hymns to the stars
> I shall love all that must die.
> And I shall walk diligently
> Upon the path assigned to me.
>
> Tonight again, the stars are blown by the wind. ('Prologue')

What characterizes the poem is the purity of thought expressed therein, which does not spare much room for moral concern in the secular sense. The poem may stand as a code of ethic Yoon Dong-Ju wanted to fulfill as a human being: being truthful to his own self while remaining grateful for having been granted life. As he watches the stars being blown by the wind, he can equate himself with any one of them that may disappear at any moment while flickering. The absolute purity of thought seen in the poem, however, is the starting point for Yoon Dong-Ju in his youthful struggle to attain unification of the two domains within himself: intellect and aesthetic sensibility. His conscience, the world of his ethic, dictates that he attain unification of the two through existential search. The Kierkegaardian notion of the fulfillment of the complete self of an individual could have influenced him, for Kierkegaard was one of his favorite authors. Most of his poems are about himself, and several of them are what one may call self-portraits. But this does not mean that Yoon Dong-Ju was a narcissist or self-indulgent man. We should rather take this as evidence of his existential search.

For Yoon Dong-Ju memories of his past are as important as the knowledge of his present self in carrying on existential search. Several of his poems deal with memories of his past. The memory of his love for Sooni still lingers in his heart, and he recaptures the moments of sadness he underwent as a young boy in 'A Snowy Map' and 'A Boy.' Although he will never be free from the memory, his past love has been consecrated in "the temple of love" and now he must carry on his struggle for self-fulfillment:

> Our temple is the temple of love
> Where ancient customs have settled for ages.
>
> . . . .
>
> Now a quiet lake in the forest waits for you;
> And rugged and precipitous mountains for me.
> ('The Temple of Love')

But, without cherishing the memory of his past, attempt at betterment of his self becomes meaningless, for his present self is an outgrowth of his past. In 'A Beloved Memory' the poet recollects how once he anxiously waited for a train that would take him to a far-away place where he would start a new life as a student. Having spent some time where he wanted to go, he now misses his former self and the moment in the past when he was waiting for the train:

> The spring has gone now—
> In a quiet rented room in a foreign land
> I long for myself—like hope or love,
> Whom I left behind at home. ('A Beloved Memory')

In 'Self-Portrait' the poet tells us how he feels both disillusioned with *and* attached to his present self. As he looks inside a well, the water reflects everything above—the moon, the clouds floating in the clear sky, and even the cool autumn breeze. When he sees his face reflected in the water, however, he turns away, unlike Narcissus, for he is not happy to see the image of his present self. But the moment he turns away, he starts missing the image, for in times to come his present self will be looked back upon with longing. The poet's reminiscence of his past is always accompanied by a longing for his former self. But his reaction to his present self often contains two ambivalent feelings—disillusionment and attachment. As he wishes to be someone much better than he is now, he turns away from his face reflected in the water. But he feels attached to his present self at the same time, for without it, he knows, his future self-fulfillment is impossible. The man he sees in the well is his present self, but he knows he will miss it in the days to come:

> Inside the well, the moon lies fair,
> The clouds are sailing in the open sky,
> And the blue wind of autumn is blowing;
>
> And there is a man—like memory. ('Self-Portrait')

The "memory" he already sees in the reflection of his present self, of course, denotes the continuity of the past, the present, and the future.

'Time present and time past are both perhaps present in time future, and time future contained in time past.' In a different context the lines by Eliot are applicable to what Yoon Dong-Ju's poetry reveals. What the poet says he has lost and tries to find in 'The Road' may be his former self. But the poem also implies that the search he carries on from day to day is not for retrogression into the past but for self-fulfillment in the future. As the poet cannot deny his former self as part of his present self, so his present life, he believes, will be part of his future self. His existential search is symbolically shown in the following poem:

> In the copper mirror, rusty green,
> My face lingers
> Like a sad relic
> Of an ancient kingdom.
>
> My contrition is condensed in a single line:
> —"For twenty-four years and a month
>   What futile expectations have kept me alive?"
>
> On a joyful day, tomorrow or the day after,
> I shall add a line of repentance:
> —"On that day, when I was still young,
>   Why did I make such a shameful confession?"

> Night after night, my mirror
> I wipe with my palms and soles;
>
> Then into the mirror looms
> The sad figure of a man alone
> Walking away under a shooting star. ('A Confession')

The rusty green copper mirror reflects not only his present self; the face lingering there "like a sad relic of an ancient kingdom" is also a reflection of his past. To see a better version of himself, therefore, he polishes it every night desperately—with his "palms and soles," lovingly and with occasional disgust. But what he sees in the mirror is "the sad figure of a man . . . walking away under a shooting star." The end-all result of his existential search, the poet knows, will be death ("walking away under a shooting star"). Yet while he remains alive he must not cease his search, his spiritual journey toward self-fulfillment. The innumerable shadows of himself he sends away ('My Shadows') belong to the past; therefore, he lets them go away to where they are due. But that does not mean that he is completely free from his past. When he makes the paradoxical statement,

> Neither have I loved a woman,
> Nor have I grieved for the times, ('The Wind Blows')

it is not to negate his past and present selves but to assert that his future self-fulfillment is still in store, despite the pain and anguish he has undergone:

> While the wind keeps blowing,
> I stand firmly upon a rock.
>
> While the river flows on,
> I am standing upon a hill. ('The Wind Blows')

The poet knows, however, that the lifelong process of self-fulfillment is not an easy one and may be cut short abruptly. Thus, when his younger brother answers that all he wants to be when he grows up is "a man" ('The Portrait of My Brother'), the poet knows the profundity of the answer his brother does not understand. After all, the goal of one's existential search is to become a man. To become a man is to fulfill one's potential. And like other existentialists, Yoon Dong-Ju was always conscious of the truth of mortality. Death may come suddenly someday and nullify all his lifelong effort for self-realization:

> On the morning when I go—after all my work—
> The leaves will fall without grieving.
>
> O do not call me yet. ('A Terrible Hour')

After all, death-consciousness is what impels one to exert his full potential during his lifetime, knowing that the end-all result of a lifelong struggle to defeat death will be another set of *memento mori*:

> Those conquerors of death,
> Who have left only their bones! ('Life and Death')

And exactly because one has to die in due time, today becomes even more precious and tomorrow is simply "another today" ('Tomorrow'). Yoon Dong-Ju died young, and none of his poems that he may have written during his last days in prison survives. But those poems that are left are enough to show us the drama of a human soul, the spiritual journey a young existentialist led during his brief life.

Yu Chi-Whan (1908-1967) was born in Choong-Mu,* a historic town on the south coast of Korea. He grew up in that town, learning classical Chinese from his father, who was a man of medicine by profession but was also a man of letters in his own right. When he was fourteen, his father decided to let him be exposed to 'new education' and sent him to Japan. While attending a highschool there, he joined a literary club organized by his elder brother,** and started

---

* The town was named after the honorific appellation for Admiral Yi Soon-Shin (1545-1598), who defeated the invading Japanese in many sea-battles around there and saved the nation far back in the Yi Dynasty. Admiral Yi Soon-Shin, who had invented the 'turtle-backed battleship,' kept his naval headquarters there. The seascape along the winding coastal line with many small isles evokes a solemn feeling in every Korean's heart.
** Yu Chi-Jin, who later became a playwright.

writing poems. After spending four years in Japan, he returned to Korea and entered Yonhi Liberal Arts College (now Yonsei University). But soon he withdrew from the college and learned photography. Apparently, he could not get adjusted to the atmosphere of a college where only the facade of academism prevailed. The fact that he was much engrossed in photography in his youth is suggestive. As a poet, it seems, he took more pleasure in capturing the moments of beauty in his camera lens than in receiving a formal college education. He opened a photo studio, but soon closed the business and devoted himself to writing poetry. His first collection of poems was published in 1939, when he was thirty-one. The next year he went to Manchuria with his family, and lived there for five years, working at a farm. The five years he spent in Manchuria as a self-exile seem to have been a period of existential search for him, for many of the poems contained in his second collection were written during this period. He returned to Korea in time to see the country regain her national sovereignty in 1945, and started a teaching career, which lasted until he died. When the Korean War broke out in 1950, he followed military maneuvers with other men of letters, although he was already over forty. When the war was over, he resumed his life as a school-teacher; and when he was forty-six, he became a highschool principal. Having published six collections of his poems in the meantime, he became a member of the Korean Arts Council in 1954. He spent the rest of his life as a leading poet, while fulfilling his duties as a school administrator. He received several awards for his poetic achievement, and was elected president of the Korean Poets' Association twice. He died of a traffic accident.

Yu Chi-Whan was a prolific writer, and during his lifetime he published a dozen collections of his poems. As he spent most of his lifetime as a teacher and school administrator, his life did not involve any dramatic events. But under the surface of a peaceful and quiet life, his inner life was a turbulent one. The reputation he attained as a poet during his lifetime does not seem to have been so gratifying to him, for he felt a vacuum in his heart all his life. Behind the appearance of poise and calm he retained, there was a man suffering lifelong solitude and groping for the meaning of his existence.

Yu Chi-Whan did not profess to be a poet. It irked him to be called a poet. He wrote poems, not because he wanted to be a poet but because he was impelled to do so. Writing poetry was not a profession for him, but a vocation. As we reflect on the real cause of his having written poetry, we must take into consideration the socio-political conditions he lived through. As a youth of the nation groaning under a foreign power, he had two choices: either to live and die as a man of action, as Yi Yook-Sa did, or to live a worthwhile life as a private man, remaining faithful to his own self. Thus, when Yu Chi-Wan went to Manchuria in his early thirties and lived there for five years in self-exile, it was not only to get away from the bleak conditions in the peninsula, but to put himself in a trial situation— to encounter the unabated ferocity of the elements on a wide-open land and attain existential awakening. His early poems thus are a manifestation of his existential search. What impelled him to write poetry was a desire to instil in his compatriots the spiritual vigor, the unvanquishable will to carry on life even in the harshest conditions. His self-imposed mission made him write, not for self-gratification but for self-fulfillment.

Striving for assertion of life in its perennial sense, Yu Chi-Whan had a soul that could not be confined within the poetic mannerism of his age created in imitation of western poetry and characterized by shallow sentiments and petty poetic conceits. For him poetry meant the task of confronting the universe, of probing into the meaning of human existence, of asserting the continuity of life-force. Throughout the corpus of his poetic writings one notices an obsession with the grand cosmic order and man's place in it. His poetry often reveals the communion between his microcosm and the macrocosm. The immeasurable solitude of a soul born into the boundless expanse of time and space is often the theme of his poetry. Thus, commenting on the presence of the cosmic providence, he once made the following observation:

I admit that God exists. But the god I recognize is not a being that will grant me any further grace than that I am alive today. He is simply the will that makes the cosmos exist in the boundless expanse of time and space. He exists not as a being that can be envisioned but simply as the will that pervades the universe— without any purposefulness—an immanent will, if you like, of nothingness. When I cease to be, he will remain unaffected. Even if this planet becomes shattered, it will be an insignificant incident for that absolute will. The ultimate wisdom we must attain, therefore, is to realize that the fate of mankind is delegated to us. . . . If I ever acknowledge the grace of God in the course of my life, it must be a sycophant gesture on my part in the presence of that cold will.

What is implied here is somewhat reminiscent of the Hardian conception of the immanent will. When Yu Chi-Whan declares his creed that the universe exists as a vast vacuum quite indifferent to human existence, he sounds almost nihilistic. But his nihilistic view of human existence is the very starting point in his lifelong struggle to confront the universe face to face and finally to assert the meaning of the precarious human existence in the cosmic scheme. Thus his poetic vision encompasses both the grandeur of the universe and the nobility of the human soul in its struggle to have a glimpse of the cosmic grandeur:

> In a single grain of sand
> Rests the whole universe,
>
> And in a single star twinkling
> The vicissitudes of a millennium.
>
> In the boundless universe,
> O this infinitesimal life of mine!
>
> But as a being so infinitesimal,
> How light-hearted I can be! ('Life')

"How light-hearted I can be!" says the poet. That light-heartedness he has attained comes from the relief brought by the knowledge that he is only an infinitesimal being in the boundless universe. But that does not mean that the infinitesimality of his life renders him an insignificant being, for "in a single grain of sand rests the whole universe." His life is comparable to a single grain of sand; but in it the whole universe can be contained. It is a paradoxical statement declaring the communion between his microcosm and the macrocosm.

Then what was the medium of that communion? One of the recurrent images in Yu Chi-Whan's poetry is the wind. In his poetry the wind is emblematic of the cosmic providence; and it works as a medium of revelation through which the message of the grand cosmos is conveyed to him. As it is insubstantial (as 'airy nothing'), the wind also stands for the vast vacuum called the universe. As the poet listens to the wind blowing from "where time and space cross," he feels the presence of a cosmic principle. It is the moment of communion between his soul and the universe. The wind touches every object that lies on its way, but it journeys on without lingering to attach any special meaning to the encounter. It is symbolic of the indifference of the cosmos to human (and subhuman) existence. The communion between the poet's soul and the cosmic spirit thus necessitates that the former converge into the latter. Throughout his poetry we detect his wish to assume the nonchalance of the wind. For Yu Chi-Whan, the wind was not merely a part of the phenomenal nature. It was a medium, a revelation of the cosmic spirit.

Then what was the message he got through this medium? With his all-seeing eyes of a poet, he saw complete nothingness in the boundless void of the universe. All sentiments, including anger and grief, were only human and, therefore, trivial to him, for all the bustle of terrestrial life becomes insignificant in the boundless void keeping sempiternal silence. But it does not mean that terrestrial existence is to be looked upon nihilistically. It rather means that earthly life is to be cherished with passionate zeal, the more because it is transitory. Thus the 'nihilism' in Yu Chi-Whan's world-view leads to passion for life and compassion for all that must die. The spiritual vigor and the will to live through hardships that he wanted to share with his compatriots are manifestations of his zeal for life. His nihilistic view of the universe led him not to pessimism but to affirmation of life, no matter how transient and painful it may be. In his poetic world there is no room for petty conceits or sentiments or indulgence in mellow verbal music. Many of his lines contain the voice of a prophet announcing the everlasting continuity of the primal force of life.

His affirmation of life, of the primordial life-force, however, often leads to indictment of the absurdities found in human institutions. The following poem may be read as his vehement indictment of institutional conventions and man-made laws:

Standing on the rebels' graves no one looks after,
The entangled weeds are laughing in anger.

As you were human in all your nakedness,
You had to bear the cross of the original sin
And be thrown like curs upon this Golgotha.
Cruel are the whips of vengeance
Slashing those who would not hear
The grandiloquent sermons on laws and ethics;
Yet your scornful refusal to pay homage
To the grand masquerades of hypocrisy
Only proves your flower-red zeal for life.
—Again,
Indict the savagery of men judging men
With this silence of yours.

Since your lives were as cheap as mine,
I do not feel any lingering regret
For your being so neglected even by your kin.
My brothers who went ahead of me!

Someday your souls shivering in the cold
May be standing at the gate of salvation,
Sobbing like orphans in grief and fear—
Only this makes me rue.

The rejection you have suffered in this rotten world
Let the dry weeds laugh at in bitter contempt.
                              ('At a Prison Cemetery')

Those who blindly honor the institutions of human society may feel
disturbed by the blatant reversal of the conventional ethic implied
in the poem. But the anger expressed in the lines is directed not
only to the human society where men deprive their fellow human
beings of their lives. The poet's indictment of the presumption per-
petrated in human society, as manifested in carrying out 'justice'
according to man-made laws, is ultimately extended to an indictment
against the cosmic providence that allows it to happen. All this, of
course, stems from Yu Chi-Whan's passion for life, his deep-rooted
love for all creatures that share life.

    Yu Chi-Whan's ideology, if he ever had one, was not a pre-
conceived system of thought, however. It was his natural reaction

to the realities of human existence. As one who retained a lifelong zeal for life, Yu Chi-Whan had to become a critic of the absurdities observable in human society. His nihilism was not a simple pessimism or a negation of life. Paradoxically, it was an attempt on his part to reach an affirmation of life. The skepticism he retained may seem non-Christian; but it means that his soul could not be bound by the yoke of any frame of thought. His poetic vision, which enabled him to see the essence of the created world in the boundless void defying both time and space, led him to an insurmountable passion for earthly life—transitory yet precious for its transience—a humanistic zeal for life of here and now.

Cho Ji-Hoon (1920-1968) was born in a family with scholarly tradition, and he learned classical Chinese from his grandfather in his childhood. When he was sixteen, he came to know several scholars devoted to the revival of Korean studies during the Japanese reign, and was initiated into what was to become his lifelong field of study. When he was eighteen, he was mature enough to attend the funeral ceremony for Kim Dong-Sahm,* held at the residence of Han Yong-Woon. Han Yong-Woon was one of the thirty-three men who read the Declaration of Independence on March 1, 1919, and initiated the historical nonviolent national uprising, which was bloodily suppressed by the Japanese police. He was a renowned Buddhist monk and poet. Cho Ji-Hoon's initiation into Buddhist philosophy is to be ascribed to his meeting Han Yong-Woon at the funeral ceremony for Kim Dong-Sahm. His poetic career was opened when Chung Ji-Yong, a leading poet of the 1930s, recommended one of his poems

---

*Kim Dong-Sahm (1879-1937) led an army that fought for national independence. The armed resistance legion under his command fought the Japanese in Manchuria, and in several battles defeated them. While remaining the commander of the legion, he was also devoted to the education of Koreans living in Manchuria and to protecting their civil rights. He was arrested by the Japanese, and after eight years of imprisonment he died at Mapo Prison in Seoul. At the time of his death, which followed a weeklong refusal to eat any food, he left the following will: "What need is there for one who is deprived of his nation to have a grave? When I die, burn my body, and throw the ashes into the Han River. My soul will linger around the peninsula till it witness the downfall of the Japanese imperialists and the rise and prosperity of my dear country."

to be printed in *Moon-Jang*, a major literary journal in those days. He was barely twenty when he started publishing his poems in the journal. After graduating from a college in 1941 he became an instructor of the academy in Wol-Jung-Sa, a famous Buddhist temple. While teaching there, he read much in Buddhist philosophy, and a year's experience of living in the temple left much influence on his poetry. When he was twenty-two, he became a member of the lexicographical society organized for a dictionary of the Korean language. His serious research on the Korean language and culture started when he participated in that project, which was soon interrupted by the Japanese police. When the nation was liberated in 1945, he devoted himself full-fledgedly to studying the cultural history of Korea and to rehabilitating proper use of the Korean language—a grave task that he, together with other scholars of Korean, had to assume, for during the Japanese reign Koreans had been deprived of their right to use their native tongue even in their private daily lives.

Having taught Korean language and literature and the cultural history of Korea at various colleges, Cho Ji-Hoon became a professor of Korea University in 1948; and until he died he taught there for two decades. During the Korean War, he organized a group of men of letters to follow the military maneuvers, and witnessed numerous battles. A few years before the war broke out, he had published a selection of his poems in an anthology entitled *Chung-Rock-Jip* (literally, "The Book of the Green Deer"), which also contained the works of two other poets, Pak Du-Jin (1916-   ) and Pak Mog-Wol (1916-1978). The first collection of his poems was published in 1952, and before his death he published three more. While teaching at Korea University, he participated in numerous social, cultural organizations and societies, and in many cases he was either the organizer or a key member. But, most of all, he is to be remembered as the one who built the Institute for Research on Korean Culture in Korea University; and it was his lifelong project to edit and contribute to *The Cultural History of Korea*, an ambitious and epochal work in seven volumes, published by the Institute. In addition to being a poet and university professor, Cho Ji-Hoon was a socially-active man. The innumerable posts he kept while leading an academic career prove that he was keenly aware of the social obligations an intellectual should assume outside the ivory tower. Cho Ji-Hoon was a stern critic of the times. During the oppressive regimes of the 1950s and

1960s he did not hesitate to criticize governmental policies and administrative flaws openly. He was a man of learning, of poetic sensibilities, and, most of all, of moral integrity.

Cho Ji-Hoon's early education was in classical Chinese, and his poetry reveals much influence of the flow of verse in the classical Korean poetry in Chinese. The artistic sensibilities underlying his poetry are genuinely Korean. In his poetry three elements are intricately woven together: austere moral deeply rooted in the Confucian ethic, transcendental vision retained in the Buddhist world-view, and typically-Korean sentiments. Cho Ji-Hoon was a nationalist, and his love for the cultural tradition of Korea lies at the heart of his poetry. At the same time, he was a man endowed with artistic sensibilities that could respond to a wide range of thoughts and sentiments, both eastern and western. But as an aesthete, he was deeply engrossed in the beauty he saw in Korean life and culture. Despite his socio-political interests, which made him an active spokesman of the intellectuals of his times, Cho Ji-Hoon did not use poetry as a vehicle for his socio-political thoughts. In his poetry we see a sustained effort to rediscover and reconfirm the beauty and the *esprit* of Korean life and culture. Cho Ji-Hoon seems to have equated writing poetry with the task of exploring the beauty of what lies at the heart of Korean culture. His attempt to rediscover and reassert the innate beauty of Korean cultural heritage was propelled by his nationalism; but it was also a natural outgrowth of his love for beauty and a desire to find aesthetic meaning in each moment of his life. Underlying his love for Korean culture and ways of life was his contemplation of the essential beauty of human existence itself.

In depicting the beauty of a certain object or of a certain moment in life, he does not provide much explanation; but he somehow lets us see the beauty and share his exultation in it. It all comes from his being able to remain 'artless' while contemplating whatever called his attention. He can empty his mind and face the object of his contemplation with a mind clear and untinged with worldly concerns. He does not remain a mere observer of a certain object, but gets absorbed in it, till his consciousness becomes part of it. We can ascribe his being able to be transported thus into an object to Buddhist contemplation, which had much affected his spiritual life from his youth. Cho Ji-Hoon was a man for whom the mind mattered more than the heart. His poetry reveals much intellectual probing into the nature of beauty, not mere indulgence in it. Devoid of shallow sentimentalism, his poetry is a perfect fusion of intellect and poetic sensibility. Commenting on the function of art, Cho Ji-Hoon once made the following observation:

> While art for art's sake, with its yearning for a world of beauty, may help us to overcome our discontent and disillusionment with the realities, art for life's sake exists to mirror the realities, to record what happens in real life. Then, which of the two will ennoble our mundane existence? Art for art's sake, with its longing for the realm of beauty, makes us dream about better-ment of our present conditions; and thus it becomes art for life's sake in the true sense of the words. Art for life's sake, on the other hand, remains content to depict the present human con-ditions as they are, and lacks the incentive for betterment of life; hence it cannot claim to be truly beneficial to life. Therefore, the differentiation between the two, we must admit, becomes quite meaningless and even misleading.

While not endorsing the moral underlying the principle of art for art's sake, he reveals his belief that art for art's sake ultimately be-comes art for life's sake. As one devoted to building up a tradition of genuine national poetry, he chose to exclude all socio-political concerns from his poetry. A man with acute political and social concerns, he wrote poems that explore the world of beauty, the world of dream.

For Cho Ji-Hoon, the world of beauty, of art, is equated with the world of dream. Throughout his poetry runs his yearning for the world of dream. His passionate longing for beauty and truth, it seems, could find its fulfillment in the world of dream. On many occasions, he directly alludes to his dreams or to the stage of consciousness which belongs neither to the waking realities nor to the world of dream—a state of transition, so to speak, that lies between the two realms:

> In my dream I walked in the snow
> On a wide-open field, alone;
>
> And I woke up this morning, feeling
> Something like a ray, like music. ('Snow-Covered Morn')

As I recline on the window
Where dream enters the waking life
My eyelids fall like a screen.

Every slumber is sweet in spring,
For every thought turns into a dream.
('The Silver-Bell in the Yard')

The above lines specifically allude to a dream or a dreamlike state. But it is not an overstatement to say that the whole corpus of Cho Ji-Hoon's poetic writings deals with dream in a broader sense of the word. Once the poet's consciousness is freed from mundane thoughts, he enters the world of dream; and the poetic insight that enables him to see the substance of an object of his perusal or to grasp the meaning of a certain moment in his life is granted him as he enters the world of dream, the realm of poetic contemplation:

Looking at the grass waving
As a stream of wind flows on it,
I let my body be swayed
By the gentle stroke of a breeze.

Lovely incarnations of life primeval,
We talk, laugh softly, looking
At each other's languid face.

In the ripples of the flow of time
The soul, flowerlike, blooms quietly. ('Grassblades')

The above lines depict a moment of sudden glimpse into the essence of phenomenal nature, a moment of revelation. As he feels that his "soul, flowerlike, blooms quietly," he is approaching spiritual awakening, the ultimate goal of Buddhist contemplation. His intellectual probing into the nature of beauty unseen by the common eyes thus necessitates that he enter the world of dream, a waking dream, in which his mind's eye becomes open to the realities of a higher order.

In the poem quoted above the lines stating the opening of his mind's eye contain the metaphor of a flower blooming:

In the ripples of the flow of time
The soul, flowerlike, blooms quietly.

Indeed, the image of flowers abounds in Cho Ji-Hoon's poetry. As
so many of his poems allude to flowers, it will not be necessary to
provide illustrations of the flower imagery. All that is needed here
is to say that in his poetry flowers function as a medium of spiritual
awakening. Flowers help the poet to realize the limitations of the
actual experiences in our physical life, and thus become the guide
to the realm of a higher order, the world of beauty and truth, the
world of dream. The moments of beauty in life or in the phenomenal
nature can be grasped only by those who have a yearning for beauty,
who want to become beautiful in the perennial sense of the word;
and Cho Ji-Hoon seems to have thought that it is important for us
to have a glimpse of the innate beauty of life, of the phenomenal
nature, if we are ever to attain spiritual awakening:

> The secret yearning of the flowers
> That bloom and wilt by themselves
>
> Only the candle knows
> That wears a white halo.
>
> Hardly audible is
> The falling of the petals;
>
> My ears are ever attentive
> For fear they fail to hear. ('Falling Petals')

In this poem Cho Ji-Hoon is not praising the physical beauty of the
flowers. Rather, he finds the essence of their beauty in their "secret
yearning" that they retain while they "bloom and wilt by themselves."
The flowers, so the poet says, are beautiful—not because they look
beautiful, but because they have a longing for permanent beauty,
although they have to wither in time. Only the candle wearing a white
halo knows the flowers' secret yearning. The candle is the poet's
sole companion, and therefore it shares his anguish for not being
able to hear the falling of the petals. The poet wishes to hear the
sound of the falling petals, because *wilting* is the substance of the

flowery existence, as much as *blooming* is. And the poet's ever attentive ears reflect his longing to enter the world of the flowers, the world of beauty, made permanent not by their physical existence but by their longing for beauty. Transitory as the flowers' physical existence is, their yearning for beauty is something permanent, a cosmic law. So is the poet's longing to enter the world of the flowers. As the above poem clearly indicates, flowers are thus a poetic medium revealing the poet's love for all phenomenal nature, all that must die, and life itself. Life is transitory, and the cycle of the phenomenal nature is based on the principle of life's transience. Yet, as Shelley's poem 'The Sensitive Plant' has it, longing and aspiration for beauty and life persists, and here lies the permanence of beauty transcending life's transience.

The above speculation ultimately leads to the question of life and death. In a symbolic poem entitled 'A Dream' Cho Ji-Hoon depicts death as a realm of dream, of peace and beauty:

Opening the gate,
I entered;
It was indeed not a gate.

The whole village
Was a sunflower field;
Upon each tall stalk
A giant face was beaming.

In the forest of the sunflowers
Suddenly thousands of cocks
Started crowing in bright daylight.

Upon the ridgeway
Overlooking the blue sea
A flower-bedecked bier
Was being carried, quietly.

On the shore a lone boat
Was floating, with many-colored silk sails
And a big drum at its prow.

An aged sire with white beard
Was reclining on the gunwale,
Playing a flute.

The flowery bier was set on the boat.
When the boat was sailing away,
Sudden darkness fell upon the sea,
Only the starlights showering upon it.

Closing the gate,
I came out;
It was, after all, not a gate. ('A Dream')

The poem abounds in the imagery of light and bright colors, and most of all, of flowers. Although "sudden darkness fell upon the sea" as the boat carrying the flowery bier was embarking upon its journey, the vision the poet had up to that moment was anything but a scene of darkness and gloom. In his dream the poet had a glimpse of the realm of death, and what he saw in it was a peaceful scene: a village in the midst of the sunflowers beaming in the bright sun, innumerable cocks crowing in broad daylight as if singing hymns to life, and a flower-bedecked bier being carried to a boat with many-colored silk sails and a big drum. Even the old man (the messenger of death) does not look grim or threatening: he is playing a flute, reclining on the gunwale, as his white beard is blown by the wind. Death, as conceived by Cho Ji-Hoon, is thus not a realm of hideous decay and darkness where all that one enjoyed in life ceases to exist. It is rather a land of dream, of perfection, that one is to enter at the end of his lifelong pursuit of beauty and truth. It is the scene of flowers. The usual conception of death as a state of annihilation and gloom is rejected here. The poet wishes to envision death as the consummation of life, not as a reversal of life. This wish reflects his strong will to accept death not as the termination of life but as a state where all that he has longed for during his lifetime is to be fulfilled finally. Thus even the dividing line between life and death is negated:

Opening the gate,
I entered;
It was indeed not a gate.

Four Modern Korean Poets

. . . .

> Closing the gate,
> I came out;
> It was, after all, not a gate.

For Cho Ji-Hoon, death was not an 'undiscovered country from whose bourn no traveller returns,' for he could freely have a glimpse of it in the form of a dream. In this poem he refuses to accept life and death as two completely different states of being. The usual conception of death as a state of nothingness, a state where all that one enjoyed in life is to be annihilated, is thus totally rejected. This kind of transcendental vision is after all a manifestation of the poet's strong will to attain self-fulfillment in the poetic realities. Ultimately, the poet finds solace in the belief that the loss of his physical life will result in an attainment of the poetic realities, far more permanent and truthful than the realities of the empirical world.

Cho Ji-Hoon's contribution to the cultural heritage of Korea is indeed remarkable. Living in an age of much political and social turbulence, he tried to get at the roots of Korean culture and spiritual life; and his life long search for beauty in what constitutes the foundation of Korean culture and life made him a poet with a unique sense of beauty and a transcendental view of life. He was a man who had an all-encompassing outlook on life and death, on the whole world, while being deeply engrossed in exploring the beauty of Korean life and culture.

Sung-Il Lee

Yi Yook-Sa (1904-1944)

Holograph MS of Yi Yook-Sa's 'The Sea' (p. 47)

Flowers

When in the East the sky has ended
And no raindrops bless the land,
Flowers bloom, redder than ever—
The days of toil to weave my life!

In the freezing dawn on an arctic tundra,
Deep in the snow the sprouts stir,
Waiting for the legion of swallows—
A promise not to be broken at last!

Where the waves foam far out on the sea,
In a castle of flowers ablaze in the wind,
Memories throng like dreaming butterflies.
Today I am conjuring you here.

Yi Yook-Sa

The Wild Plain

On the primeval morn,
When the sky was dawning,
Somewhere indeed a cock crew loud.

When all the mountains
Were rushing to the ocean with longing,
They could not invade this wild plain.

Through endless time
Seasons bloomed and faded diligently,
Till a vast stream found its way at last.

Now snow falls
And plum-blossoms' fragrance fills the air,
Here I am sowing my scanty seeds of a song.

After an infinite flow of time,
He who arrives on a white horse
Shall sing it loudly upon this plain.

A Monologue

My face bleaching like cold mica
May look imbued with the shade of death,
For I am standing under the moon.

My shoulders higher than a mast's
Tower above the web-like clouds;
And I hear the wind and the waves below my ears.

Lonesome as a wandering seagull,
How can I know my journey's end?
I let my thought drift on a flag.

As the cabin windows are draped in blue
And the candle drips, melting in nostalgia,
The canal bears its nightly rainbow.

Spreading a pair of wings like a bat
In the gloom of a cloudy night,
I shall rise to gleam in the air.

Shall I fade away when the cocks crow?
As the white mist spreads at dawn,
I shall descend to flow with it.

Yi Yook-Sa

[33]

The Sea Waves

A strange sound approaching quietly
As a maiden stepping to her bridal chamber!
Knowing no one will call me tonight,
I open the window to hear the waves.

What intruder is this—besieging
The night of a lone turtle-backed isle?
Who is rattling the door to my treasure
Without my permission, ruler of the isle?

Louder than the hooves on the Caucasus plain,
It draws nearer and nearer—a presumptuous marauder!
What can I surrender, except my passion,
A poor exile paling on this isle?

Rushing ashore so stout-heartedly,
Why are you out of breath like a smuggler?
Are you imploring with your pent-up anger,
While in my castle the night is deepening?

The steps of the prisoners dragging the chains—
An eerie sound reviving a memory!
Is the night's pledge to regain freedom
Being renewed in whispers before the dawn?

A sound strange like the cry of the nuns
In black veils! Is the sobbing at my feet
Of a lovely maiden running from a convent
Tonight, when my wrath is swelling like the waves?

A strange sound—when no one would call me!
The moan of a lion dying from a thunderbolt?
With the last roar closing your life of grandeur
Break the mossy castle of this isle!

A scream of the throes in a labor room!
Let's wait for the baby to be born tonight.
Ah, the strange sound! Dashing in with roars,
It keeps the isle awake through the night.

A choir celebrating the birth of a giant!
A song of jubilee reaching to the heavens!
The waves sing of autumn to soothe me,
And call my soul. O the sound of the waves!

Yi Yook-Sa

[35]

Evening Glow

I open the curtain of my small room
To receive the evening glow like a guest.
As the seagulls flying above the waves,
What loneliness men have to bear!

Stretch your soft hand, evening glow,
For me to rub my burning lips.
Let me send my kisses to all
You are embracing in your bosom—

The stars of the twelve constellations,
The nuns in prayer after the evening bell,
And the convicts shivering in cold cells—
For their poor hearts are trembling in loneliness.

Let the caravan toiling on a desert
And the naked savages living in a jungle,
While resting in your warm embrace,
Receive the blows from my burning lips.

Though my room is warm in May,
I'll open the curtain tomorrow again,
For like the sound of a brook fading,
The sunset does not retain its glow.

My Muse

My Muse in his tattered rags
Has not yet seen a glorious day,
And has held his reign at night only.

Despite his utter penury,
Assuming the world is within his sway,
He even flies to the kingdom of Indra.

He does not tell where he was born;
But he is proud of having been reared
In the nipping winds of a northern seashore
And having travelled on the back of a whale.

His beard forbids him to indulge in women;
And, when drunk, he walks the luring alleys,
Covering his large white ears with his cloak.

But banqueting with me beside the fountain
Where melted jade has flowed for eons,
He sings heartily with his unchanging voice.

When the night is wearied and the cocks crow,
He ascends the starry stairs in big strides.
Now the candle is out, I fall asleep,
As the dew-laden lilies lean on my sleeves.

Note: While the Muses are female in Western literature, the poet conceives
      of his Muse as a male figure, in accordance with his poetic spirit.

Yi Yook-Sa

[37]

Opium

A languid night on a southern isle—
A bonfire burns at a banquet.

A soul colder than a gem
Is drawn to the streets where the measles blow.

While another Noah's flood sweeps,
A star twinkles above the perilous isle.

Come, bring your naked body,
Like a sail swelling with the spring breeze.

The splendor of life dazzling like a rainbow—
A world worth to live, while sinning.

My Song Flew Away

On a moonlit night in mid-December
When the stream froze and stopped flowing
The song I had sung flew over the river.

To where the sky meets a desert
My song flew away like a swallow.

The poor runaway dear to my memory
Flew away on its little wings
To certain death on the burning sand.

The desert beneath the endless blue—
Night will descend on it as the teary stars mourn above.

Night sprouts memory lovelier than a rainbow.
Leaving its echo here, where has the strain gone?
The song I had sung flew over the river.

Yi Yook-Sa

[39]

Lake

Suppressing the urge to rush out, the lake,
Lulled by the wind, regains its pensive eye.

Once in a while it calls the swans to fly;
But, hugging the shore, it turns to sob at night.

While it nibbles on the faint starlights,
Purple mist descends on it like a veil.

Green Grapes

July is the month in my home
When the green grapes ripen.

The legend of the village mellows in clusters,
And the dreamy sky settles in the beads.

As the sea bares her bosom to the sky,
A white-sailed boat will come adrift,

And my longed-for guest will finally arrive
With his weary limbs draped in green.

Feasting on the grapes to welcome him,
I shall be happy to wet my hands.

Prepare at our table, dear boy,
A white kerchief on a silver tray.

Yi Yook-Sa

Eclipse

Once as a child I held an ink-spread tray,
And saw the monster eating up my only sun.

Night after night I had prayed it would prove a lie
That the sun, the moon, the earth, all stand in a line.

At last in the cavelike dark my heart fluttered—
A rosebud, before it bloomed, was eaten by a worm.

But wasn't it the lovelier, being so short-lived?
I shall find another sky somewhere,
And cherish it in the dewy starlight.

A Tall Tree

As if to touch the blue sky,
The tree soars above the flame of time,
Bearing no flowers even in spring.

Draped in old webs,
It indulges in an endless dream
With a heart throbbing—not for regret.

Unable to bear loneliness,
Its shadow plunges deep in the lake,
Which the wind has not the heart to shake.

Yi Yook-Sa

The West Wind

Charged with a frosty beam,
You come from the deep blue sky.

After lurking on the floor of a river,
You rise to glide on the hoary reeds,
Hide in the sheath of a long sword,
And blow on the sail of a lonesome exile.

The day when a young widow looked so fair
You made the crickets chirp in the grove,
And shook the leaves to rustle in remorse.

I welcome you, wind, for you are ominous.

A Midnight Song

In my home, where countless lights should glimmer,
Graves lie moss-grown, with no butterflies around.

A dark dream swallows both grief and pride,
While in the pipe quietly burns a fragrant flame.

The smoke, drifting like a sail, settles in the harbor,
And the familiar windows are glazed with salty tears.

Life is weary without winds and snowstorms—
The footsteps of the shadows returning after bitter wine—

Within a choking heart, where can a river flow?
The moon follows the river, and the cold stream flows
    into my heart.

In my home, where countless lights should glimmer,
Graves lie moss-grown, with no butterflies around.

Yi Yook-Sa

[45]

Plantain

My feverish breath is floating today
Above the silvery ripples like the leisurely moon.

O plantain, lift your green sleeves
And sprinkle dew on my scorched lips.

On the day of the fall of an ancient kingdom
We said farewell to each other for ever.

Upon the sleeves the women clung to
Their delicate hands still weave a dream.

Whenever I see the distant stars or the blooming flowers,
I long for the days we have long lost.

We'd rather, after a thousand years,
Listen to the rain on an autumn night.

If a rainbow rises somewhere at dawn,
We shall part again, treading on it.

The Sea

When a seagull's claws scratch the sea,
The sea gives breath to the wind.
Here is the grace of the sea.

When a white sail slices the sea,
The sea only tickles the sky.
Here lies the generosity of the sea.

When old nets entangle the sea,
The sea simply engirds the land with its blue.
Here lurks the conspiracy of the sea.

Yi Yook-Sa

[47]

To a Boy

At the brink of a pond shining
With the pearls of cold morning dew
A lotus flower blooms big.

Now, boy, you are born indeed;
And nourished by a clear soul,
You will grow like a gourd flower.

The river flows with torrential sounds,
And the rapids engrave on white pebbles
The sound of the setting sun.

Riding a stallion, you will love
The spirit upright like
The bamboo sword on your back.

After strolling the streets
You may stand like a statue
Before a fountain in the plaza.

As the west wind blows on your cheeks
And the clouds float leisurely above,
You will sing of the white and blue sky.

But when the song wavers
And the stars freeze in the cold,
What if you too go mad!

Bat

Deep in the cave unblessed by light,
Or above the ruins of a castle, you hover alone,
Poor bat, prince of the dark!
The rat has deserted you to flee to a rich barn,
And the roc has long since flown to the north sea.
While your mourning for the century is being torn to tatters,
You have not tasted love that the doves find sweet.
Poor creature, spirit of solitude!

You have neither chattered like a parrot
Nor have, like a woodpecker, made an old tree sound.
Should you blame heredity for your agate-colored eyes?
Unable to chant a spell, you grind your teeth in anguish.
Having lost your nation and your perch, you have nowhere to go.
Poor soul doomed to be a wanderer for ever!

Though not Phoenix perishing in the flame of passion,
Doesn't the Philomel crying blood-choked all night
Wring our hearts and draw tears from our eyes?

Remembering the glory of your remote ancestors,
Whose sharp claws would threaten the hinds' livers,
You now grieve over the Ainu-like decline of your clan.
Bats, a nation perishing!

Now the incense burns no more on the altar of fate,
Can you lure the birds to receive you among them?
Unable to please the eyes as some birds in the cages,
You must return to your cave without ever having a dream.
Poor creature, dark fossil of fairy dreams!

Yi Yook-Sa

[49]

Looking Back

My life is a broken bark—
Its pieces are scattered over dreary fishing villages,
And only the dust of living remains like wornout sails.

While others found their youthful days happy,
My nightly dream, like a junk smuggling over the western sea,
Was brined and swollen in the salty waves.

Every night, after escaping a reef, I fought a storm;
And where the fabled coral island could not be found,
Not even the Southern Cross shone above.

Pursued, dragging my weary limbs,
I climbed the longed-for horizon at a breath,
When the stagnant water, like tropical plants, girded my ankles.

Like a spider driven by the tide at dawn,
I've drifted here, clinging to a crumbling shell.
Looking back at my long journey dotted by distant harbors—

Let us Sing of a Star

Let us sing of a star, just one—
For how can we sing of all the stars in heaven?

Just one! The one we see at dawn and at dusk—
Let us sing of the star, close to us and the brightest.
Let us own a big star that will shine in our bright future.

To own a star is to own a globe.
Upon this earth with nothing to lose except sorrows,
Let us sing of the joy for owning a new globe
With our full throats to our hearts' content.

The fellows at night labor dreaming of young girls' eyes
And the caravan toiling on a desert, longing for a fountain,
Will have their dreams and longings come true.
Even the fire-field farmers will find their fertile acres.

Each as an owner of the rich soil of the globe,
Let us sing of the star uninhabited yet.

Upon the solid earth of the star, yet another globe,
Let us sow the seeds of plenty with our own hands.
At the banquet celebrating a rich harvest
Let us sing aloud, half-drunk and uninhibited.

As the god ruling men is an ever holy one,
He will not follow the emigrants to the new star.
Let us scatter like pearls on the new earth
A song free from the decree of retribution.

Let us sing of a star, even though only one.
Let us sing, one by one, of all the stars in heaven.

Yi Yook-Sa

[51]

Yoon Dong-Ju (1917-1945)

파란 녹이 낀
구리거울 속에

내 얼골이 남어있는 것은

어느 王朝의 遺物이기에

이다지도 욕될가.

나는 나의 懺悔의 글을 한줄에 줄이자.

— 滿 二十四年 一個月을
무슨 깁븜을 바라 살아왔든가.

내일이나 모레나 그 어느 즐거운 날에

나는 또 한줄의 懺悔錄을 써야한다.

— 그때 그 젊은 나이에
웨 그런 부끄런 告白을 했든가.

밤이면 밤마다 나의 거울을
손바닥으로 발바닥으로 닦어보자.

그러면 어느 隕石 밑으로 홀로 걸어가는

슬픈 사람의 뒷모양이
거울속에 나타나온다.

一月 二十四日.

懺
悔
錄

Holograph MS of Yoon Dong-Ju's 'A Confession'
(p. 65)

Prologue

Until I breathe my last breath
I wish to face my sky without shame.
Even a wind blowing on leaves
Has left me restless.
With a heart singing hymns to the stars
I shall love all that must die.
And I shall walk diligently
Upon the path assigned to me.

Tonight again, the stars are blown by the wind.

Yoon Dong-Ju

[55]

A Snowy Map

This morning when Sooni is leaving
Snow falls in large flakes upon my grieving heart,
Covering the map stretching far outside the window.
The room is empty, for I am alone.
The walls and the ceiling are all white—
Is it snowing even in this room?

Are you going indeed—as someone of the past?
What I wanted to say before you leave
I would write in a letter, but cannot post it,
Not knowing where you are going, where you will live,
In what street, in what village, under which roof—
Is my heart the only address I know?

I cannot follow your small footsteps on the snow,
For snow keeps falling, covering all.
When this snow melts,
On each step you left a flower will bloom.
When I look for your footsteps among the flowers,
In my heart there will be a yearlong snowfall.

A Boy

Here and there the autumn drifts,
Sad as the withered leaves falling.
Having prepared the spring to return
To each twig whence the leaves fell,
The sky stretches far above.

The boy intently looks at the sky,
While its blue settles on his brow.
He rubs his warm cheeks with his palms,
And finds they have been tainted in blue.

As he looks into his palms, wondering,
He sees a river flowing therein,
A clear stream along his palm lines;
And within the stream looms a face
Sad as love—the face of Sooni.

The boy closes his eyes in rapture;
Yet the river flows on,
Wherein lingers the sad face,
The lovely face of Sooni.

Yoon Dong-Ju

A Beloved Memory

One morning when spring was coming
I was standing at a small station,
Waiting for the train—like hope or love.

I was casting a thin shadow
Upon the platform, smoking.

My shadow blew the shadow of the smoke,
And the pigeons flew, unashamed
Of the inside of their wings in the sun.

The train, bringing no new hope,
Only carried me far.

The spring has gone now—
In a quiet rented room in a foreign land
I long for myself—like hope or love,
Whom I left behind at home.

Several trains, bringing no one,
Must have gone already today.

Even now he must be loitering
Upon the hill near the station,
Waiting for one who is not coming.

—Ah, youth, stay there long.

A Poem Easily Written

The night rain whispers outside the window
Of this rented room in a foreign land.

Knowing a poet is a creature of sad fate,
Shall I compose a few lines?

Having received the money from home
That brings the smell of sweat and love,

I walk to the classroom with a college notebook
To listen to the lecture of an old professor.

Having lost my childhood friends,
All of them, one after another,

What am I still looking for,
While I sink in the stream of life?

When living a life is hard, as they say,
To write verses with ease is a shame.

In a rented room in a foreign land,
While the night rain whispers outside,

I light a candle to push out the dark,
And wait for the morn to come like an age.

I offer myself a small hand—
The first handshake that brings tears and comfort.

Yoon Dong-Ju

[59]

The Temple of Love

Sooni, when was it that you entered my temple?
When was it that I entered yours?

Our temple is the temple of love
Where ancient customs have settled for ages.

Sooni, close your crystal eyes like a doe;
I shall tidy up my hair tangled like a lion's mane.

Our love was of the mute.

Before the flame dies on the sacred candle-holder,
Sooni, run apace to the front door.

Before the dark and the wind knock at our window
I shall walk away through the back door,
With a heart swelling with our eternal love.

Now a quiet lake in the forest waits for you;
And rugged and precipitous mountains for me.

Primeval Morn

It was a certain morn—
A morning not yet tainted
By spring, summer, autumn, or winter—

When a red flower suddenly bloomed
In the gleam of the primeval sun.

It was the night before—
Yes, it was the night before—
That all preparation had been made

To send love along with the snake,
To let poison grow in a little flower.

Yoon Dong-Ju

Self-Portrait

Turning around the curve of a hill,
I walk alone to the well beside a paddy,
And look inside quietly.

Inside the well, the moon is fair,
The clouds are floating in the clear sky,
And the cool autumn breeze is blowing;

And there is a man looking at me—
I turn away, not wanting to see him.

While I walk, I feel sorry for him;
I go back—to see him still there.

I turn away from him again;
As I walk, I start missing him.

Inside the well, the moon lies fair,
The clouds are sailing in the open sky,
And the blue wind of autumn is blowing;

And there is a man—like memory.

Returning at Night

As if retreating from the world,
I return to my small room,
And turn off the light:
To leave the light on
Can be very tiresome,
For it prolongs the day.

Now I want to open the window
To let in some fresh air.
But it is dark outside
Just like this room,
Or the world, for that matter;
The road I took in the rain
To get back to my room
Is still wet with the rain.

Unable to wash away
The mortification of a day,
I close my eyes—
When I hear a brook
Running within me:
Now my thoughts are ripening
By themselves, like apples.

Yoon Dong-Ju

A Terrible Hour

Who is calling me there?

In this shade where withered leaves look green,
Here I am still breathing.

Is there still room in the heavens,
And are you therefore calling me,

One who has never raised his hand,
One who has no heavens to look up to?

On the morning when I go—after all my work—
The leaves will fall without grieving.

O do not call me yet.

A Confession

In the copper mirror, rusty green,
My face lingers
Like a sad relic
Of an ancient kingdom.

My contrition is condensed in a single line:
—"For twenty-four years and a month
    What futile expectations have kept me alive?"

On a joyful day, tomorrow or the day after,
I shall add a line of repentance:
—"On that day, when I was still young,
    Why did I make such a shameful confession?"

Night after night, my mirror
I wipe with my palms and soles;

Then into the mirror looms
The sad figure of a man alone
Walking away under a shooting star.

Yoon Dong-Ju

The Cross

The sunbeams that followed me
Are now falling on the cross
At the steeple of a church.

How can one climb up there,
To the steeple so high?

Now the bell is not ringing,
I shall loiter awhile, whistling.

If the cross is to be granted me,
As it was once to Christ,
One who suffered gladly,

I shall quietly endure,
Drooping my head,
While my blood oozes like flowers
Beneath the darkening sky.

The Wind Blows

Whence is the wind coming,
And whereto is it going?

While the wind blows,
I suffer for no reason.

Do I suffer for no reason, indeed?

Neither have I loved a woman,
Nor have I grieved for the times.

While the wind keeps blowing,
I stand firmly upon a rock.

While the river flows on,
I am standing upon a hill.

Yoon Dong-Ju

[67]

Walk with Your Eyes Closed

Dear children, who long for the sun,
Dear children, who love the stars,

Walk in the dark
With your eyes closed.

While you walk,
Sow your seeds.

If a stone hits your feet,
Open your eyes, quick and wide.

The Road

I have lost something.
Not knowing what I have lost and where,
With my both hands groping my pockets,
I walk out into the road.

The road runs along a wall,
Stretching on long lines of stones.

With its iron-gate firmly closed,
The wall throws a long shadow upon the road,

And the road runs on—
From morning to evening, and to morning again.

Leaning on the wall, while tears are welling,
I look up to the sky that baffles me with its infinite blue.

I keep walking on this bare road,
For I am still on the other side of the wall.

I live on from day to day,
For I am still looking for what I have lost.

Yoon Dong-Ju

My Shadows

Standing at a corner of the dusky road,
I strain my day-weary ears
To listen to the dusk moving.

Am I so gifted
As to hear the footsteps of dusk?

Now I have understood all, alas, too late,
I send away one by one
My innumerable shadows, that have suffered long,
To where they are due.
Into the dark around the corner
My shadows walk away silently.

These dim shadows—
The long-cherished shadows of mine!

After sending all my shadows away
I return, empty-hearted, through an alley,
To my room slowly sinking into dusk,

Where I shall stay calm and peaceful—
Like a lamb indulging in daylong grazing.

A Blessing
—From *St. Matthew*, Chapter 5, 3-12—

Blessed are they that mourn;
Blessed are they that mourn;
Blessed are they that mourn;
Blessed are they that mourn;
Blessed are they that mourn;
Blessed are they that mourn;
Blessed are they that mourn;
Blessed are they that mourn;

For they shall mourn for ever.

Yoon Dong-Ju

The Cosmos

The clean-looking cosmos
Is my only dear lady.

When the moon shines chilly,
I walk to the cosmos garden,
Unable to suppress my longing
For the girl dear to my memory.

The cosmos becomes shy
At the chirping of the crickets;

And, standing before the cosmos,
I become shy as when a young boy.

The cosmos and I share one heart,
For, though twain, we are one.

The Portrait of My Brother

As cold moonbeams settle on his brow,
My brother's face is a sad portrait.

I stop walking
And hold his small hand:
—"What would you like to be when you grow up?"
—"A man."
His answer is terse and tart.

I let go his hand
And look into his face again.

As pale moonlight bathes his brow,
Indeed his face is a sad portrait.

Yoon Dong-Ju

A Wonder

After pulling off all covering my feet,
Shall I try to tread on the lake,
As dusk does, spreading over it?

Indeed it is a wonder
That I was drawn to the lake,
When no one called me here.

Today
Longing, complacency, and envy
Cling to me like cumbersome medals.

Now I want to have all these
Washed away in the water,
Please summon me onto the lake.

Forest

A heart shrinking with the ticktock of the clock
The forest calls.

The forest darkened for a thousand years
Is ready to embrace a life-weary one.

From above the black waves of the forest
Darkness weighs down on a young heart,

And the evening wind shaking the leaves
Makes me tremble with fear.

The distant croaking of the frogs in early summer
Evokes the memory of an old village.

Only the stars twinkling through the trees
Lead me to hope for the coming days.

Yoon Dong-Ju

Mountain Top

Now I have come up to this mountain top,
The streets look like the lines of a chessboard,
And the river winds like a little snake.
By now people
Must be spread like chess pieces.

The midday sun
Shines on the zinc roofs only.
And a train creeping slowly
Stops at the station, and starts moving again,
Coughing up black smoke.

Lest the sky like a tent
Collapse upon the town,
I feel like climbing up higher.

Tomorrow

People kept talking about tomorrow;
So I asked them what it is.
They told me that tomorrow will be
When night is gone and dawn comes.

Anxiously waiting for a new day,
I slept through the night and woke up
To learn that tomorrow was no more—
It was another today.

Friends,
There is no such a thing
As tomorrow.

Yoon Dong-Ju

Both

The sea is blue;
So is the sky.

The sea is boundless;
So is the sky.

When I throw a stone into the sea,
It only smiles.

When I spit on the sky,
It remains quiet.

An Encounter

I was walking up the hill,
When three beggar-boys passed by me.
The first one was carrying a basket, slung over his shoulder,
Filled with empty bottles, tin-cans, metal pieces, dirty socks,
    and what not.
So was the second boy;
So was the third.
Their shaggy hair, sooty faces, blood-shot eyes with tears,
    discolored and pale lips, threadbare patches covering
    their loins, and bare feet bleeding—
Ah, what dreadful penury has swallowed up these young boys!
Pity welled up in me.
So I searched my pockets—
A thick wallet, a watch, a handkerchief. . . .
But I had not the courage to part with them;
I only felt them in my pockets, wondering what to do.
Having made up my mind to limit my charity
To having a friendly chat, I called, "Hallo, boys."
The first one turned his bloodshot eyes to me;
So did the second one;
So did the third.
Then, whispering among themselves, as I was an intruder,
They walked away down the hill.
The hill was empty,
While the dusk was falling upon it.

Yoon Dong-Ju

Until the Dawn Comes

Wrap in black garments
Those who are dying slowly.

Dress up in white clothes
Those who are still living.

Then upon the same bed
Let them lie side by side.

If they weep for hunger,
Soothe them with human milk.

When soon the dawn comes,
The trumpet sound will be heard.

Life and Death

Even today life sang a prelude to death.
When will this song be over?

While we live,
We dance to the song of life
As joyful as to melt away our bones.
While we live,
We are unable to remember
The horror to follow when the song is done,
When the sun finally sets over the hill.

Who was it that sang this song
As if to engrave his name in the sky?

Who was it that stopped singing
As suddenly as a shower stops?

Those conquerors of death,
Who have left only their bones!

Yoon Dong-Ju

Yu Chi-Whan (1908-1967)

Holograph MS of Yu Chi-Whan's unpublished
poem, 'Wind among the Pines'

Thus Spake the Himalayas

Only those who brood
Can endure this immense solitude,
For eternity
Knows all, yet rejects all.

Peak after peak, in an endless array,
I am soaring on this edge of the world.
Against the roaring storms slashing me
I am standing where dawn and dusk converge.

You who cried, "Eli! Eli! Eli!"
Forsake the race you could not herd;
Come rise with me here
In a frozen statue of sempiternal solitude.

Yu Chi-Whan

Midday of Life

Midday aflame in the scorching sun—
See what an ecstasy has immersed them all,
All the creatures in the bliss of life.
The cicadas are indulging in their daylong singing,
And, unable to contain their springing vigor,
The wild beasts are fallen asleep somewhere.

Now none of the creatures in life's fellowship
Is being meddlesome or fearful of others,
As all, with their mouths buried in their breasts,
Are greedily sucking life's nectar.
Even if they drink it up to the last drop,
There will be nothing to regret, after all.

Midday aflame in the burning sun—
The sky and the earth are overflown with a soundless song.
See what an ecstasy has made all creatures drunk,
While they roll and revel, hugging their lives.

The Chapter of Life

When my learning is unable to withstand the onslaught of doubts
And I can no longer bear the burden of love and hate,
While striving for life like an ailing tree,
I shall leave for the faraway desert of Arabia.

There the sun rises to glare in godlike grandeur,
And the sand has buried all in sempiternal silence.
In that vast desolation Allah alone
Keeps nightly vigil in unshared agony.

When I stand all alone in a wind-flapped garment
In the midst of the soul-cleansing solitude,
I shall be brought to face myself, as if my fate.
If I do not thus regain
The primal state of my being, my life,
I shall not rue my bones bleaching on the sand.

Yu Chi-Whan

Treading on the Fallen Leaves

Treading on the fallen leaves,
I walk in the wood on an autumn day,
When suddenly I feel sorry for myself.

Once a year the trees, emptying themselves
Of all their thoughts, profusely shed
These dazzling golden poems.

But I, who have toiled for forty years,
Have not yet poured out a single grief.

Beneath the sky so clear and blue,
One who remains ever vexed with cares,
And those who lead a quiet life, contemplating—

O the difference!

The Sky at Night

That is an ocean, indeed—
Ready to receive me into its wide expanse.

Day after day,
When I return from my work in the evening,
It draws nearer and nearer my window,
Spreading the sounds of the wind and the waves.

At this corner of the vast expanse,
Upon a sand bar breeding only meager thoughts,
I am arduously collecting
Only empty shells.

A flicker from an isle
Deserted in the farthest nook of the expanse
Is already more neighborly to me
Than the earthly island of Tahiti or St. Helena.

Indeed an ocean,
An ocean I shall have to cross someday—
So I live on at this obscure shore,
Waiting for my turn to launch into it.

Yu Chi-Whan

[89]

Life

In a single grain of sand
Rests the whole universe,

And in a single star twinkling
The vicissitudes of a millennium.

In the boundless universe,
O this infinitesimal life of mine!

But as a being so infinitesimal,
How light-hearted I can be!

At a Prison Cemetery

Standing on the rebels' graves no one looks after,
The entangled weeds are laughing in anger.
As you were human in all your nakedness,
You had to bear the cross of the original sin
And be thrown like curs upon this Golgotha.
Cruel are the whips of vengeance
Slashing those who would not hear
The grandiloquent sermons on laws and ethics;
Yet your scornful refusal to pay homage
To the grand masquerades of hypocrisy
Only proves your flower-red zeal for life.
—Again,
Indict the savagery of men judging men
With this silence of yours.

Since your lives were as cheap as mine,
I do not feel any lingering regret
For your being so neglected even by your kin.
My brothers who went ahead of me!

Someday your souls shivering in the cold
May be standing at the gate of salvation,
Sobbing like orphans in grief and fear—
Only this makes me rue.

The rejection you have suffered from this rotten world
Let the dry weeds laugh at in bitter contempt.

Yu Chi-Whan
[91]

Ailing Wife

A faint smile is her answer; yet
Her closed eyes tell me she ails.
A flower blooms, fades, and withers;
So does a maiden grow, sicken, and die.
Before this cosmic law
I am as helpless as the universe,
For I am unable to share her pain.

Are you lying there with your eyes closed,
Thinking of the futility of the sentiments
That cling weblike to our fragile bodies?
Are you already listening
To the soundless wind blowing in the nether world,
While your lonesome soul is floating
Towards the vast inhabited by the stars?
Are you stretching out your thin hand
Still to feel your earthly ties?

You were once
A flower that set my youth aflame.
Through the years of penury you have been
A tree of exuberant green, in whose shade
I've found repose of love and hate.
Is it already the fall?
Is the autumnal wind already blowing on you?

When you are no more—
The mere thought renders me a grief-stricken beast.
Yet this is only a futile complaint of immaturity.
In the presence of the solemn truth,
You must go like a wind,
And I shall be left behind, a lonely wind.
You are so close to me—yet so far away!

Spring Haze

"Uh-hwa-nung, uh-hwa-nung, uh-hwa-nung-cha, uh-hwa-nung!"
The coffin-bearers' song is heard.

Spring has come to revive the earth,
And somewhere a lark is singing.
Through the haze rising from the earth,
Along the winding path in the green field
A funeral bier is being carried,
With its streamers flapping in the breeze.

The whole earth is soaked in life;
Yet here is a stern division—
Dust is to be borne to the field,
And grief is nailed in the hearts.
The heart-wrenching cruelty is a pulse in nature,
As on the same branch some flowers bloom, some wilt
Is life so? Is weeping a beautiful part of it?

After all, life is a haze.
Sad as it is, it is a haze;
Happy as it is, still a haze, a mist.
The day when you go and leave me behind!
The day when I go and leave you behind!

Yu Chi-Whan

Standing in the Dusk

Standing on the road where dusk is falling,
I feel my eyes being glazed with tears;
But I know my tears are not for sadness.

Looking at the distant mountains fading into dark,
The crescent moon throwing its beams on the road,
And the sunset clouds melting away traceless,
I feel a sudden gush of happiness—
For my being able to see them
And tell what they all mean;
Therefore, I weep for joy and gratitude.

Standing in the dusk gradually spreading,
I feel my eyes being glazed with tears;
But I know my tears are not for grief.

As the glow of the setting sun lingers above the hill
And the sound of the evening bell is spreading far,
I weep for joy and gratitude—
For being blessed with life prostrate in prayer.

Among the Pines

As I stand among the pines densely arrayed,
What causes this chill that makes me feel
A certain presence in this forest?

I look around—to see only plants and stones.
The rocks, covered with moss, kneel prostrate,
And the trees, dragonlike, wearing scales,
Soar high as if to menace the sky.
What are they ready to attend upon?

As the wind blows from where time and space cross,
What makes them wait in a solemn array
Sparing no room for the petty sentiments,
Such as loneliness, grief, and longing?
What is this presence?

Yu Chi-Whan
[95]

I Don't Know Who I Am

I don't know who I am:
Where I came from and how, I never know.
All I can tell with conviction are:
My name made up of three syllables,
The number of years I have lived,
And my abode where my body dwells.

Neither am I a child of God,
Nor do I owe my being to my parents only.
Thrown blindfold from where time and space crossed,
I am standing here like a reed on a bleak riverbank.
I can see what my poor body does
And hear the hollow echoes of my voice
Till, like sunset fading on a hill,
I shall at last turn into nothingness.
The annihilation of my being,
I know, is beyond my will.

Therefore, don't offer me a draft of tenderness;
Don't grant me a heartstring of yours.
When the time comes, your due will be
A wail Heaven itself cannot redress.
I don't know when I shall be gone, and where;
I don't believe what I think I am.

With My Puppy

"Dear Puppy, let us walk,
Let us walk together."

With my puppy beside me
I am sitting on a hill.

Tilting its head,
It watches me tenderly.

I too look into its eyes,
Its clear eyes that seem to reflect

An understanding of the sky,
The earth, the wind, and life itself.

"Dear Puppy, do you too see in my eyes
The whole universe contained therein?"

While we are blessed with life
In the midst of the creation,

We know, though mute and silent,
The meaning of a leaf fluttering in the breeze.

"Dear Puppy, do you know how we people
With our words have strayed from the truth?

"Dear Puppy, let us walk,
Let us walk together."

Yu Chi-Whan
[97]

A Wonder Was Nearby

To wait for my child coming late from school
I went out to the dusky thoroughfare,
When I saw the dreamy crescent at the road's end,
And above our home glimmering through the elm branches
The dazzling Plough was keeping guard like a sentinel.

Sometimes an ailing one brings cares,
And poverty remains an endless worry.
But look! the bliss of a simple life
Has been watched over all these nights—
Passing human life at its smallest
Is linked to the cosmos.

Dear child, come home quickly;
Let us walk, hand in hand,
To our home watched over by the stars.

Another Olympus

Dusk comes again.

The lingering evening glow dyes the distant hilltops.
While the sparrows chirp merrily under the eaves,
The father returns from his day of honest sweat,
And the children reluctantly leave their playing.
The mother, who has been busy at home all day,
Sets the table for them to sit around.
Now at dusk the poor gods are brought together.
Though not endowed with heavenly wings,
They weave the myth of the present century
By living through the tribulations of today.
Soon after their supper table is cleared,
Night will wave in to enwrap them all,
And the small divine clan will sleep in peace.

All this—long before religions ever existed!

Yu Chi-Whan

The Stone Buddha of Sokuram

Suppressing the urge to wail in grief,
I am sitting here with my eyes closed.
Within this cold stone kept for a millennium
Blood flows on as I breathe.

O life! It is—
It is not to be granted again,
Even after a billion years;
It is not to be given up so.

Wind from the distant pines,
The lotus leaves on the swelling sea,
The ear-piercing caw of the crows,
And the moonbeams falling on my forehead—
I feel all.

Who will know?
Suppressing the urge to wail in grief,
I am sitting here with my eyes closed—
A mere stone enduring eternal solitude.

Herald of Spring

Through the shady branches of a cherry
Blooming like a lamp before the window
A little bird comes to play and departs.

Having endured the bleak season of winter
With folded feathers and crouching legs
At some corner of a distant field,
Did you come drawn by this hazy spring?

The branch where it just sat and left
Is still shaking after it has flown away.
This smallest of lanes leading
Through the shades of flowers!

Yu Chi-Whan

Longing (1)

Although not an invincible regret,
I have been cherishing this lifelong grief,
As if it were my guardian saint.

In retrospect I truly feel
The heart-breaking farewell we made then
Was a good one, after all.

One may forsake a country for love's sake;
Yet for commonsense of worldly wisdom
I have bought grief, but not regret.

Reliving the moments of the heart-wrenching farewell,
I feel like wailing to the heavens once again,
Holding you in my arms yet once more.

Therefore, my cherished pearl, O heavens,
Even unto my death-bed you shall be with me,
For my life has been a long stretch of longing.

Longing (2)

It is windy today,
And my heart grieves in the wind.
Strolling the thoroughfare
Where we used to walk together,
I look for your face nowhere to be seen.
My longing grows as the wind blows,
And all day long my heart grieves
Like a flag sobbing in the wind.
Are you hiding somewhere like a flower?

Yu Chi-Whan

Night Wind

In your letter
You said you would enclose
The sound of the wind out there;
And, waking up at night, I listen.

Rushing to me from a faraway place
With a long howl of loneliness,
It takes me ten thousand leagues away.
The solitary sound!

Unable to sleep with many thoughts tonight,
Are you too lying awake till dawn breaks?

To those who do not know what longing is
What meaning can the blue of the sky have?

Indeed, the solitary wind at night
Must be blowing for you and me alone.

Howling again, unable to bear longing,
The wind blows—you are rushing to me!

Leavetaking

My well-worn briefcase in hand, I step
Into the station to be swept along with the crowd,
Having said farewell to no one.

The usual sentiments of sadness and grief
Coming over us at a leavetaking
We may as well do without.

When surging grief calls for tears,
The best greetings for such an occasion
Are silent smiles on our faces.

The wind journeys on, after touching a tree—
Like the wind, I have learned
To live with equanimity.

Yu Chi-Whan
[105]

Mountain Clouds

There they go,
The clouds go,
The mountains go.
There they go, thick and round,
The clouds and the mountains, all in one,
Nang-nim, Myo-hyang, Tai-paik, and So-paik,
All of them in one green hue,
Soaring above the tumult
Of the waterfalls and the cicadas down in the valleys.

There they go,
The mountains go.
After the splendid palace of the summer clouds,
The dazzling roll of night-silk is spread.
Rolling and tumbling is the boundless vast.
There they go,
The clouds go,
The mountains go.

Night

Night comes,
When day is done,
To bury all in darkness—
Indeed, there must be a god.

A cliff blocking my eyes, pressing the eyelids!
In this boundless void even without a sound
Where am I being held now?

When I strain my ears,
I hear someone weeping ceaselessly—
Grief welling from the depth of his soul,
A mournful cry heard from far—

Is it you, God?
Is it you who is weeping?
Even for you, almighty and self-sufficient,
Does your being, your having to endure,
Cause solitude immense as mine?

As I shall soon cease to be,
My loneliness will not last for long.
But for you, whose undying authority
Renders it impossible to cease to be,
What everlasting loneliness for you!

Yu Chi-Whan
[107]

I Will Go to the Sunflower Field

I will go to the sunflower field.
Standing in the midst of the sunflowers,
I too will become a sunflower.

With lions' mane of golden radiance,
In the posture of proud princes,
Keeping silence all day long,
Staring at the summer sky aflame,
They forbid even the butterflies to come near.

I will be with them in the sea of resolution
That spares no room for doubts and sentiments.

I will go to the sunflower field.
Standing in the sunflower field,
I will turn into a sunflower at last.

The Sea

This is all—
Even after billions of years
My heart will show only this.
Having thrown all away,
I am lying here, wide-sprawled.
Come, quickly, come.
Can you not hear this wail of grief
I cannot suppress by day or night?

Beneath the sky in its primal state
Weighing down on me relentlessly,
I can only dash and roll, wail and roar,
In regret and despair, grief and anger.
Sometimes I calm myself
And lie wide-spread in peaceful repose.
Within me, unreconciled,
Day and Night live together—
Profound and boundless love
And dreadful roars threatening the sky.

Somewhere beneath this very sky
Mountains rise to face the universe
And freeze in its eternal silence.
Come, quickly, come,
And soothe me to learn their stillness.
Until you come
I shall remain ever turbulent.
Here on these seething waves
My heart lies.

Yu Chi-Whan

A Brief Rest

Dusk falls quietly after the battle,
And we are resting at the shore of a lake.

Watching the smoke arising from your pipe,
Are you thinking of your faraway home?

Both the sentiments of love and hate
Are only human, after all.

The scenery left behind by our enemy
We are enjoying in peaceful repose.

As a Wild Flower

Where the battle swept last night
Like a nightmare,
A young enemy soldier is lying dead,
Lonesome as a wild flower.

Pursued like an animal,
You were driven at last through this gate.
Now the cruel storm of life has passed away,
How peaceful you are here!

Now you will hear,
For the ear of your soul will be open,
The distant roar of the East Sea
Resounding into eternity.

Yu Chi-Whan

Life and Death

Lamps put aside—flameless!

Only a few minutes ago
They ran out like happy deer—

Aren't they pretending to be sleeping?

No. Life was, after all,
A futile game that couldn't last long.
Now they may have gone back to whence they came.

With their faces covered by white sheets,
Lieutenant Paik tilts his head a bit to the left,
And Sergeant Wu keeps a leg on Lieutenant Paik.

Between what was so painfully hard
And what is now so easy

Here is no difference any more.

On a Battlefield

Knowing at any moment
A flying bullet can end his being,
Each feels life and death
As no more than a passing wind.
O this calm—

It is not because their lives are
As cheap and common as the pebbles on the road.
For each of them his life
Is more precious than the whole world,
And each one is embraced in unfathomable love.

But look—
How carefree they are,
As if their being alive or dead
Were no more than a passing wind!

Unless one has trodden this path—
If one has learned only to cling to his life—
What if he would write a score of books!
They are but a heap of trash—
Contempt is all I can bestow on him.

Yu Chi-Whan
[113]

Sunset

The setting sun throws its beams on the starving village.
The setting sun throws its beams, bright and beautiful.

No smoke rises from the chimneys of the village;
The children and the aged have fallen asleep in hunger.

Having no meals to conclude the day,
The villagers are all out to see the setting sun,

For among them are still those
Who can be lords and sirs, as in olden days.

Like a gift from the heaven, the setting sun
Throws its beams on the quiet villagers.

The Skylark

Try to listen
To the skylark singing.
Far beyond the edge of the field,
Somewhere in the sky fading in haze,
The lark is singing all day long.

The distant peaks that stood menacing
Swell like a wavy roll of purple silk.
The fragrant breeze blows,
Caressing what lies on its way.
The once dried-up brooks sing,
And the grassy field begins to stir,
As the young sprouts are ready to burst.

Try to listen,
For the lark is singing
A song of joy for the return of life.
The lark is singing,
For spring is here to revive the earth.
If you listen with your eyes closed,
What a song! It will move you to tears.

But here
Is a valley where spring never comes—
A valley sad, desolate, and cold,
Where men groan, striving for life,
Only to despair and die, hugging together.
In this valley inhabited by men
When will that dazzling song be sung?

Yu Chi-Whan

Try to listen
To the skylark singing.
The lark is singing deep in the haze
With its full throat all day long,
For spring has come to the field and the stream—
Spring that never comes to the valley of men.

At an Orchard

One night
The Holy Spirit visited the Virgin Mary;
So these virgins
Fully grown to receive the Spirit,
Cherishing their lovely dreams,
Cast their eyes up to the sky,
Quietly stretching their limbs in anticipation.

Whence and how will the dove-like spirit come?
Will it come with the sunbeams?
With the wind?
With the faint starlight at night?
Or will it come as a youth?

One does not need to know,
For no one knows how the Holy Spirit came to the Virgin.

Their sacred mission, their only wish,
Is to be wedded by the unknown Being
And bear babies with apple cheeks—
After the Virgin blessed by the Holy Spirit.

This is a cloister not to be defiled—
Numberless virgins awaiting the holy impregnation
Are reverently stretching their lovely limbs.

Will the Spirit come
With the sunbeams?
With the wind?
With the starlight?
Or will it come as a rocky young man?

Yu Chi-Whan

The Song of a Tree

Being lonely is not true loneliness;
Having to endure it to the end is.

O Time, how idly you have
Given me youth and taken it away
To leave me standing here alone.

O winds, birds, that come to nestle on me,
While you are with me, find all the pleasure you can;
Yet you will never reach deep within me.

O star, star of mine,
Offering prayers to your altar every night,
I grow in the dark seven times as tall.
As I endure the countless days,
Standing in the winds blowing on me,
How can they know my secret yearning for you?

I shall cherish this loneliness;
I shall ever remain tall alone.

Eagle

You were born somewhere on the surging waves.
You are a drop of the deep blue of the sky.
Little soul, that soars high
In the clear air of July,
Proud as you are,
Away from the animal passion for the earth,
Away from the grovelling worries love and ties bring,
Away from the sordid world men rule,
Carrying your stern yet carefree soul,
You fly in the boundless sky,
Held by no anchor but your serene thought.
Your dazzling dreams are spread wide
Upon the wings that soar above the world.
—Ah, the eagle!

Yu Chi-Whan

Bat

You were born to crawl.
What makes you then abhor
The earth and the daylight
And hide under the roofs of deserted houses,
While gossamer fancy and eerie dreams
Eat up your body?
Why the wings
That flutter under the pale moon
While you dance alone sadly?

Enemy

Weary of the pathos of love,
I'd rather think of my enemy.
Where are you now, my dear enemy?
I wish to give you a hearty kiss,
For I have always been righteous and strong
Only in the presence of your daggerlike malice.

Yu Chi-Whan

To the Wind (1)

O wind, I know—
I know what your message is.

Why you shake the grass
And, after touching my face,
Wail in the sky, I know—
I know what your message is.

When I close my eyes, lying on a hill,
You come even to the depth of my soul.
In the midst of the vast universe,
O my Mona Lisa,
How much I long to embrace you!

O wind, I know
Why you sob upon a grass-blade—
I know indeed what your message is.

To the Wind (2)

O wind, it may be that
I am standing on your way
While you make your solitary journey.

O wind, it may be that
My heart is a wall with a chink
You pass through on your journey.

O wind, I hear you,
Lying in the dark
This sleepless night.

At the Crossway

The telegraph pole is howling.
Standing alone on a wide-open field,
It is howling in unbearable loneliness.

Lean your head to listen to me,
For I am like the telegraph pole.

In the endless flow of time
A chance crossing of eternity and infinity
Made me born into this boundless void.
Listen to the howl from the depth of my soul.

Although only a lifeless log,
The telegraph pole is howling.
It is howling in my stead.

This is Why I Write Poems

Do you know why the peddlers
Yell and bellow so loudly?

Do you know why the children
Cry with such ear-piercing voices?

Do you know why the stage conductors
Twist their bodies and limbs so much?

Do you know why the musicians
Keep blowing and scratching and beating?

Do you know why the winds
Keep wailing and howling like crazy?

Do you know why the waves
Never learn to stay calm?

Do you know why the mountains
Have lost their voices
And finally become so quiet?

Do you know indeed why every object
Tries so desperately
To empty its heart with a cry?

Yu Chi-Whan

When I Die

When I die, shake me once more, to see if I wake up, before your bury me.
Suppose I wake up in my grave—what horror and despair will come over me!

O Eternity! Everlasting nothingness!
At last unable to measure you with my life,
I shall fail to grasp the meaning of your emptiness,
And lie down like a bird fallen on the ground.
Yet you won't be disturbed—mountains, universe!

The last song I shall sing,
The song nobody would hear,
The song I shall loudly sing all alone!

At Last I Shall Know

At last I shall know
It has all been an emptiness.
I am like a nameless flower
That blooms and dies, unseen in the field.
I shall know when the time comes
My tormented life full of anguish
Has been only a gust,
A patch of cloud that leaves no trace.
Life is not to be granted again—
On the night when I cease to be,
I pray you, sun and moon,
Do not throw your beams upon my body;
Let the firmament embedded with countless stars
Be my grand tomb for eternal repose.
The suppressed crying of the grass insects
Will be my wail of grief over unfulfilled wishes.
At long last I shall know
It has all been a vast emptiness.

Yu Chi-Whan

Cho Ji-Hoon (1920-1968)

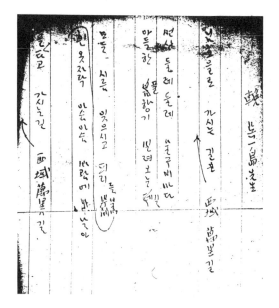

Holograph MS of Cho Ji-Hoon's 'The Going'
(p. 138)

When I Play the Flute

When I play the flute, sitting in the pavilion,
I hear a crane call amid the clouds.

Drenched in the dew is the green grass;
The pale moon sinks below the hill.

Like the wind flowing over a stream,
The cold white clouds overflow my heart.

When I play the flute, reclining in the pavilion,
The flower-rain and the flower-wind mingle with my tears,

And the twelve peaks of Cha-ha are seen,
Where a deer weeps, chewing the soft sprouts.

Cho Ji-Hoon

Snow-Covered Morn

Should I open the curtain to know
Snow covered the mountains during the night?

Underground the tender roots
Of the daffodils already know.

Deep into the night, myriad thoughts
Gathered to the lamp like moths.

In my dream I walked in the snow
On a wide-open field, alone;

And I woke up this morning, feeling
Something like a ray, like music.

In a generous spirit to embrace all,
The snow fell, shaking its head,
To cover the earth with its warmth.

Without opening the curtain I know
Snow covered the mountains last night.

Grassblades

Below the ruins of an ancient wall
Is a rock weathered in the flow of time.

I climb the hill and stand on it,
As the sailing clouds beckon far.

Looking at the grass waving
As a stream of wind flows on it,
I let my body be swayed
By the gentle stroke of a breeze.

Lovely incarnations of life primeval,
We talk, laugh softly, looking
At each other's languid face.

In the ripples of the flow of time
The soul, flowerlike, blooms quietly.

Cho Ji-Hoon

A Minstrel

Upon the lone path winding through
The surging field of barley and corn
A lonesome traveller is walking,
As if blown on with the midday clouds.

The tobacco-pouch and the spectacle-case
Are hung snugly from his belt.

The outer garment soaked in the rain
That fell during the windy night,
Bundled with the socks and the pipe,
Is slung lightly over his shoulder.

Near the rock by the sobbing brook
Below a sad pile of wishing stones
He rests his legs and closes his eyes
To pick the strings of his cherished harp.

The little girl who used to follow
Barefoot in threadbare clothes
Of handsomely matching white and purple
He has buried in the alder-filled valley.

The dusk falls upon the road
Creeping to the hill overgrown with pines.
His white beard is blown by the breeze,
As the lonesome traveller walks in sorrow.

The Pagoda

Like a woman rising
From the water, turning
To put on her clothes,

The pagoda stands
Drenched in the moonlight.

The fragrance of the grass lingers
On her body glittering in the moon.

Whenever the dark wood shakes its shadow,
Her hair waves, flowing down her shoulders.

As I approach quietly,
Longing to see her white face,
Surprised, she turns her head away,
And looks at the distant hill, shyly.

Did the moon slipping out from the clouds
Have a clear glimpse of her?
Wherever I stand, her back turned to me,
She always hides her face.
O pagoda!

Suddenly she
Spreads in the air
A roll of transparent silk,
And winding it around her body,
Starts walking quietly
Toward the wood.

Cho Ji-Hoon

[135]

Step after step,
Ascending the stairs,
I watch the moon declining
Over the woman's dark hair
As she walks away.

Around her slender waist
The streaming wind flows
Like a brook.

A Dream

Opening the gate
I entered;
It was indeed not a gate.

The whole village
Was a sunflower field;
Upon each tall stalk
A giant face was beaming.

In the forest of the sunflowers
Suddenly thousands of cocks
Started crowing in bright daylight.

Upon the ridgeway
Overlooking the blue sea
A flower-bedecked bier
Was being carried, quietly.

On the shore a lone boat
Was floating, with many-colored silk sails
And a big drum at its prow.

An aged sire with white beard
Was reclining on the gunwale,
Playing a flute.

The flowery bier was set on the boat.
When the boat was sailing away,
Sudden darkness fell upon the sea,
Only the starlights showering upon it.

Closing the gate,
I came out;
It was, after all, not a gate.

Cho Ji-Hoon
[137]

The Going

The journey is taken all by himself—
A long journey of ten thousand leagues.

Along the streams winding through
The meadows and the hills far away

The lingering fragrance of the green grass
Follows him on his long journey.

His white garment
Is fluttering in the breeze,

As he plays a willow pipe,
Having left all his cares behind,

On his journey over the setting sun,
A long journey of ten thousand leagues.

Feeling the Autumn

The winds already
Sound like celluloid being rumpled.

The sky is clear and blue,
Ready to ring like a xylophone.

When I feel like holding a brush
To put a red dot on the blue,

No wonder the fruits ripe to the core,
Having absorbed the sunrays all summer,

Turn red outside,
As they mellow.

Their single-hearted will to ripen
Till they burst and drop their seeds

Has come to fruition under the sky.
Upon that blue expanse—

One or two clear dots!

Having worked through a busy season,
Now I feel like sitting by the window.

A time when one feels the urge
To sit and reminisce quietly,

Autumn is the season
When fallen leaves cover the roots.

Chi Ji-Hoon

[139]

While the sky is getting higher and higher,
My heart remains calm and serene;

In the crisp, clear winds
The calico suit smells fresh.

The Silver-Bell in the Yard

In the yard
The silver-bell is ringing.

"The baby must be awake."

Opening the window, I see
Dewdrops rolling down the leaves.

"Dewdrops rolling down the leaves
Make so big a sound?"

As I recline on the window
Where dream enters the waking life
My eyelids fall like a screen.

Every slumber is sweet in spring,
For every thought turns into a dream.

While memory fades into a dream,
I hear girls laughing.

"Could be the sound of the brook running."

Feeling sudden brightness on my closed eyes,
I thought the sun was rising;
But it was a peach-blossom cloud blooming.

Ah what was it that drew me
To the window this morning?

As a mountain bird flies away,
The shade of the flowers shakes.

Cho Ji-Hoon
[141]

A Dialogue

"I go out to the field when the cock starts crowing,
And come home, washing my hoe in the moonlit brook.
Do you know what it's like?

"On a straw mat spread in the yard
I eat my supper with my poodle beside me.
I snore, lying wherever it happens to be,
And play the bamboo flute whenever I want to.
Can you feel what it's like?

"Wrapped in the clouds, I plow the field
With my old wife, who then looks pretty.
After a rain I go to the stream
To catch fish with the kids.
Will you laugh and call it a primitive life?

"Of those who leave home with puffed-up ambition
None comes back in good shape.
What other wishes can I have
Than that the seasons will keep
Their time, year after year?

"Let those in office do their job all right,
So we can live in peace—
I have no other wishes.
Do you know what I mean?"

The old man closes his eyes;
And then making a broad smile,
He pours for me a bowl of *makkoli.**

* *makkoli:* The most common drink of Korean peasants,
brewed from rice malt, tasting a bit tart and crude.

"Well, I think I know
The taste of this, at least."

O green mountain, and white clouds,
I have a mouth, but not much to say.

Cho Ji-Hoon

"Here Lies an Enemy Soldier"

From Ui-Sung to An-Dong, then to the Jook-Nyong Peak,
The maneuver drives on like a sweeping wind.

I jump down from the truck to quench my thirst,
And fondle a chrysanthemum blooming nearby,

When I see a piece of wood stuck in the grass,
With a scrawl in white chalk—

"Here lies an enemy soldier."

Beside it, the body of a young boy,
Whose life is still lingering in his feeble breath.

His blood-soaked limbs are already rotting,
And his half-open eyes have lost their luster.

Dragging your bleeding limbs, you must have crawled
Here to dip your head and drink long.

Within the same motherland
The soil of your home must smell the same.

Even though you were an enemy,
Even if you had not been of the same blood,
The mere thought of shared life made someone write this!

Who can perpetrate further butchering
Upon your soul seeking peace now?

As if bidding farewell to a beloved one,
I am leaving you,
My heart still staying behind.

Beneath the clear blue sky of autumn
The battle goes on, while

A piece of wood is standing quietly,
Bearing the grief lovingly engraved on it—

"Here lies an enemy soldier."

Cho Ji-Hoon
[145]

At Dabuwon

After a month's siege we come out to Dabuwon,
Where thin clouds are strewn over the hills.

This is the place that has been torn
By the howling cannons for a whole month.

All this time Dabuwon
Has remained so close to the town of Taegu.

For a small village to be kept
Within the bosom of a free motherland

Not even a single annual plant
Could run its full course of life.

O do not ask—
Why this scene of havoc
Was necessary, after all.

The trunkless head of a battle horse
Still screaming in silence to the sky—

An enemy soldier lying on the roadside
As if sobbing in self-reproach and remorse—

Heaven once allowed them all
To move blessed under the same sky;

But now in the chilly autumn wind
They are spreading the smell of mackerels.

If fate is not to be blamed for this,
If we cannot believe it should be,
What solace is there for these deaths?

Dabuwon revisited by the survivors
Gives no repose to the dead or the living,
While the winds keep blowing.

At Doriwon

A battle that drove us to the gate of death,
Once over, was no more than a passing storm.

The burnt cottages
And the flattened huts—

A village turned into brands and ashes
Today I go by nonchalantly.

Heaven has granted a special grace
To an old crock that remains intact.

This fragile earthenware reminds me
That my life still goes on even today.

The villagers return in ones and twos,
And on the empty site look at the hills.

Above the villagers the sky is blue;
And in the autumn sunrays at Doriwon

The cosmos are blooming,
Shivering in the cold.

The Road

I walk together with Time, who can never leave me behind.

But Time does not drink. I stop at a tavern once in a while; and, if I fall asleep after having a few drinks, Time walks far ahead of me, waiting for me to catch up with him. I get up hurriedly, and run after him, till I find myself a bit ahead. Panting, I fall to the roadside.

Another Time called Tide runs to me to help me rise up. I resume my walk quietly. Time, who fell behind, having finally caught up with me, flops down on the grass. Time and Tide start talking together in whispers. I walk far ahead of them, waiting for them to follow me.

Now it is natural for me to stop at a tavern, for I have to have a drink again. Once inside the tavern, I drink, watch people arguing and fighting, raise my own voice for some reason, get seized by the collar, and then sing a song smartly to my heart's content. By then the sun is already setting.

Yet another Time brings to me a small piece of paper. "Must be the will of Time dead!" I open the paper; written therein, I find a song I sang for him once.

Moonlit Night

Dangling from the eave spreading its wing unto the sky,
The windbell is ringing in the breeze.
Through the lightly drawn bamboo screen
The moon sheds her beams unto this ethereal night
Deepening with the song of a philomel.

O beautiful—what other words will do now?

The snow-white collar of her azure garment
Reflects the silvery moonbeams.
Her long gown flowing on her limbs
Glitters like a stream in a moonlit night.

Like a butterfly fluttering
As if to tell a long-forgotten tale,
Dance softly, lightly,
With your moonbathed forehead downcast.

Tonight, I am an ancient bard;
To the lyre I am playing with my eyes closed
Wave your slender arms like the tender branches
Of a dancing willow.

At an Ancient Temple

While beating a wooden bell,
Unable to fight off drowsiness,

The pretty altar boy
Has fallen asleep.

The statue of Buddha seated high
Smiles silently.

Along the road to the west
Stretching over ten thousand leagues,

Beneath the dazzling glow of sunset
Peony blossoms shed their petals.

Rain on the Plantain

The lonesome cloud that floated away,
Where will it rest tonight?

As the sparse raindrops
Fall on the plantain at dusk,

I open the window
To face the green mountain.

As the sound of water never tires me,
My longing for the mountain grows ever.

The cloud that fleeted away in my morning dream,
Where will it rest tonight?

Night

There comes a night
Hushed as if someone is calling.

There comes a night
When soft rain quietly falls
To lull my soul.

Spreading my pale fingers
In the dim candlelight,

I rub my eyes in the incense-filled air,
Though tears are forbidden on such a night.

Living in the air,
The birds ever worship the sky,
And fly far above the clouds.

There comes a night
When the wind caresses my face
Resting upon the window-sill.

Cho Ji-Hoon
[153]

Falling Petals

The secret yearning of the flowers
That bloom and wilt by themselves

Only the candle knows
That wears a white halo.

Hardly audible is
The falling of the petals:

My ears are ever attentive
For fear they fail to hear.

Even the Philomel is wearied out
After a night's full-throated singing.

It grieves me to fall asleep
On such a night—alone.

A Song from the Cave

As my body wanes,
My soul grows richer.

I drink from the well
The moon and the stars have melted in.

Pursued, I have come alone,
Trying to soothe the wounds,

Still feeling the sharp blades
Wielded by my reckless youth.

Yet knowing that, after all,
I have done well to live on,

I weep,
Plucking the grass.

Run through a wide plain,
My dreams, even today.

In the deep mountains
Leaves are falling.

Cho Ji-Hoon

When I Stand on a Hill

When I stand on a hill overlooking the sea,
I am only a wretched animal.

Life ever fades away,
Hiding behind the clouds,

And hungering after flesh and blood
That haunt me even in dreams,

I am still
A suffering animal.

Like a clam lying on the sand
To bathe in the bright sunbeams,

Like a crab, a poor ghost
Wandering among the dark graves,

I shall someday be swept away
By the awesome waves rushing.

I am an animal who's yet to learn tears,
When I stand on a hill overlooking the sea.

Village

Along the lone path
Through buckwheat flowers

A flock of sheep follows
The white moon rising.

Having lost his willow pipe,
The boy who keeps the cow

Lies on the grass
To watch the sky.

That above the mountain
White clouds bloom and die

The girl who picks cotton
Has forgotten.

Cho Ji-Hoon
[157]

Shadow

Standing by my window in the dark,
Who is looking into my room?

Who is he that watches me
With his heart-piercing eyes in silence?

All my sins glimmer phosphorescent
In the pitch-dark night when the whole world is awake.

On countless nights when I sweat in anguish
Someone watches me, standing by my window.

Who is he that watches me night after night,
Yet at dawn when I slaughter all thoughts of my sins

And open the window as if to open my heart,
Walks away sadly into the dark? Who is he?

Silent Night

On the yard I swept clean, worrying
If my steps would disturb
The starlight showering,
From the tree falls
A single leaf
Silently.

Cho Ji-Hoon

Longing

As my beloved is far away,
My heart is grieving; yet

As I have one to long for,
My heart is light.

None will boast plenty of tears
This sad life draws from the eyes;

Until my beloved comes, however long,
I shall not lose my quiet smiles.

Let my fleeting life be buried in clay
To bloom and wilt where my beloved will pass.

Should I thus meet my beloved again,
Prompt withering would not grieve me.

Ah, a lovely star shining
In the dark of night—

Put on a Crown of Thorns

Take off your gem-bedecked crown,
And put on a crown of thorns instead.

Walk out of your beloved ivory tower,
And tread on the rugged path of barren soil.

On this road where neither birds sing nor flowers bloom
Let the holy beams from your halo fall.

Tears will turn into dew wetting the grass,
And the righteous sun will shine in the sky.

Let your generous soul
Be a blessing to this turbid world.

Your voice calling out for me
Ever rings in my ears;

But I am yet unable to return,
Despite your incessant beckoning,

For I am bound by your law to stay upright
In the midst of evil, while tasting the bitter cup.

You who ever befriend the weak,
Tread on this thorny path barefoot;

Lead me into the waste land
Where I shall wail loudly.

You have taught me to carry the burden
Of all the evils and the world's pain;

Cho Ji-Hoon
[161]

To cleanse my sins away I shed tears
Of self-reproach before the groaning multitude.

Poesy, my light, my guardian spirit!

Precepts

Stand against the ill-gotten power
Trampling your meek and gentle heart.

In a world that calls a deer a horse,
Detest your shameful docility
Making you pretend to agree.

Spit on your feigning to be aloof
While barley becomes beans in their lies.
A rugged stone invites the chisel?
Well, a round stone rolls to fall.

Don't allow the sick times to embrace you,
But sharpen your conscience
Against the blades of the minims.

First of all,
Fight your own polluted mind,
Indict the evil in your heart;

And then wail.

Cho Ji-Hoon
[163]

Walking Alone

"I shall not talk any more."

Having cleared my chest
Of the words buried therein,
I walk home with an empty heart,

When the sunset looks so lovely.

The cool breeze instills sadness,
And growing hunger leads me to a tavern.

"I shall not talk any more."

Those who were attentive and nodded in approval,
All of them are gone now.

What is left at the end
Is always walking home alone.

Envy, betrayal, and conspiracy
Chase me like a shadow;
Yet I don't have a single enemy
Who may help me to forget loneliness.

"I shall not talk amy more."

Though I haven't lost anything,
I feel tired for some reason.

Suppressing the urge to shout at the air,
I direct my unsteady steps to go home,

When the long-forgotten moon of Li-Po
Floats in the sky, beaming.

The Road to Light

Sharing the mountain paths with wild beasts,
I drink the water welling under the rocks,

When the tune of a reed reaches my ears,
Spreading the joy of life from yonder hill.

My pupils that daily resemble the sunflowers
Are like two bronze incense-burners.

To the sun rising above the East Sea
I shall outpour all my griefs.

When my feet injured by rocks and thorns
Are fully cured to tread on the flowers,

I shall feast myself with songs and dances,
Picking the fruits ripening on the trees.

The song I sing on my way to the light
Will be a gust of wind sweeping my griefs away.

Cho Ji-Hoon

An Afternoon at the Zoo

When I feel overridden with sadness,
I go to the zoo.

The grief I cannot share with others
I want to impart to the animals.

"I am not here to watch you."
I feel like crying, rubbing my cheek against them.
"The poems I write with secret zeal
No one would care to read."
Continuing my steps along the gratings,
I read the poems I wrote and collected with care.

Suddenly it is I behind the bars.
Lifting my eyes, I see
Everywhere, through the partitions,
The foreign animals watching me.

They are whispering,
"Here is a poet without a country."

An afternoon at the zoo, and the scene is reversed—
The setting sun casts its hue sadly.

At a Tailor's

Surrounded by four mirrors, I feel lost,
For I see so many versions of me.

When I finally find one who looks like me,
To the right there are twenty-three more;
To the left I see twenty-three more.
But each of them looks different from the others.

Which one is the true reflection of me?
The one in front of me steps forward alone.
I know there are many hiding behind me;
But when I turn round, they disappear.

When I face my real self, I shall feel sad.
I love myself—who is not the real me.

Cho Ji-Hoon
[167]

The Soul's Home

Like a sunflower turning ever
To the flowery sun aflame,
Let the soul worship the lofty sky
And find a home in the clear palace.

A flower smiling over the thorny bush
Blooms, drenched in the dew of tears.
Let corporeal pain be gladly endured,
For the soul lives in the consecrated home.

If a smile can be born from suffering,
Grief and pain become precious.
Only those who love suffering
Can wear the halos of the soul's beauty.

Like a lark soaring ever
Unto the sky, higher and higher,
Let the soul worship the clear sky
And find a home in the lofty palace.

On a New Year's Morn

Even though the whole world falls into utter confusion,
The starry movements follow their decrees,
For unto the world inhabited by men
Another new year's morn is come.

Of the everlasting flow of time
That knows neither a beginning nor an end,
Who dared to attempt division
And call a spot the New Year's Day?

There have been, since the primeval morn,
Regrets for unfulfilled wishes.
Is another new year's morn come
For men to whip themselves
With renewed resolutions
To persist in their dreams?

Another year will pass,
While we are pondering over
The old and the new, right and wrong, life and death.

As the purple sky opens up above the soaring mountains,
As the burning sun rises above the surging waves,
So open, so rise,
O the morn for renewed dreams!

Cho Ji-Hoon

[169]

Sounds

When I close my eyes, standing in the sun,
My ears become wide-open.

The sounds I hear as my ears open
Are like songs of the bright rays.

The sound of the wind spreading on the field,
After crossing the snow-covered mountain,
Is light green.

In it I hear the sprouts and the leaves
Whispering among themselves.
It brings the sound of a willow pipe.

The breeze flowing over the paddies,
Along the hedges and the clay fences,
Is yellow—

The color of a butterfly fluttering
Over dandelions, golden bells, or fences.
Isn't it a warbler that I hear?

The wind in the mountains far and near
Howling as it sweeps on them
Is light crimson tinged with purple,

The color of azaleas, peach or apricot blossoms,
Of a festive day for all the villagers.
Suddenly I hear a chorus of the national anthem.

As I open my eyes, I hear no sound;
As I shut my ears, I see no color—
Only withered branches and frozen earth.

But spring is already in winter.
Grass, flowers, and fruits,
All are hidden under the ice.

Always dreams are one step ahead
Of the season in our waking life.

When I close my eyes, standing in the sun,
I see a world bathing in bright rays.

Appendix:
Ten Additional Poems

Translated by Lee Insoo

Note on the Translator:

Lee Insoo was born in Korea in 1916, and studied English literature at University College in the University of London, where he received the degree of B.A. Honours in 1940. He was a professor at Korea University until 1950, when he was killed soon after the outbreak of the Korean War. A pioneer of English studies in Korea, he translated poetry both from and into English. He was the first Korean scholar to translate twentieth-century English poetry, including T. S. Eliot's *The Waste Land*, into Korean. He translated more than fifty modern Korean poems into English, many of which have been published in journals and anthologies.

The Vertex

Lashed by the bitter season's scourge,
I'm driven at length to this north.

Where numb circuit and plateau merge,
I stand upon the swordblade frost.

I know not where to bend my knees,
Nor where to lay my galled steps,

Nought but to close my eyes and think
Of winter as a steel rainbow.

Yi Yook-Sa

[175]

Primeval Morn (2)

Where the snow lies white,
Over the howling telegraph poles,
The voice of God is heard.

What revelation?

With haste,
When spring comes round,
Will I enact my sin,
And wake to pangs in store.

And after Eve's travail and toil,

Hiding my shame with fig leaves,

I will endure the sweat on my brow.

Yoon Dong-Ju
[176]

Counting the Stars at Night

Up where the seasons pass,
The sky is filled with autumn.

In this untroubled quietude
I could almost count these autumn-couched stars.

But why I cannot now enumerate
Those one or two stars in my breast
Is because the dawn is breaking soon,
And I have tomorrow night in store,
And because my youth is not yet done.

Memory for one star,
Love for another star,
Sorrow for another star,
Longing for another star,
Poetry for another star,
And O! Mother for another star,

(Mother! I try to call each star by some such evocative word,
names of school children with whom I shared desks, names of
alien girls like Pai, Kyung, Ok, names of maidens who have
already become mothers, names of neighbours who lived in
poverty, names of birds and beasts like pigeon, puppy, rabbit,
donkey, deer, and names of poets like Francis Jammes and
Rainier Maria Rilke.)

They are as far away
And intangible as the stars.

Mother!
You too are in the distant land of the Manchus.

Yoon Dong-Ju
[177]

Because I have a secret yearning,
Seated on this star-showered bank,
I have writ my name thereon
And covered it with earth.

In truth, it is because the insects chirp
All night to grieve over my bashful name.

But spring shall come to my stars after winter's delay,
Greening the turf over the graves;
So, this bank that buries my name
Shall proudly wear the grass again.

Yoon Dong-Ju
[178]

Another Home

The night I came back home,
My bones that followed lay in the self-same bed.

The dark chamber was one with the universe,
And the wind blew down like a voice from heaven.

Looking into the bones
Quietly bleaching in the dark,
I know not whether it is
Myself that weeps, or my bones,
Or my beauteous soul.

The upright dog incorruptible
Barked all night at darkness.

He who barks at darkness
Must be hunting after me.

Let me go away, away,
Like a person pursued,
Unknown to my bones,
To yet another home of peace.

Yoon Dong-Ju

Flag

Behold that voiceless shouting to the sea!
That handkerchief of ever-yearning heart,
Waving unto the distant purple sea!

Elected pathos, wavelike, flaps in the wind,
And on the staff of the pure and pointed thought
Sorrow outstretches, like a heron, its wings.

Ah! Can no one tell me who it was
That first knew thus to hang into the air
This grieving heart, the plight of being?

Yu Chi-Whan
[180]

Rock

Let me become a rock after death.
Neither tainted by pathos of love,
Nor moved by human mirth and wrath,
But as carved by the wind and the rain
In the sempiternal silence of passionlessness,
Lacerated deeper and deeper,
Till at last my very life is obliterated;
Even as the sailing cloud,
Or the distant thunder,
A rock will I be,
Neither singing in dreams,
Nor crying with pain, though cleft in twain.

Yu Chi-Whan

Sun of My Life

Shall not the bright sun shine
Above my head where'er I go?

Abiding by the ancient primitive laws,
Be it my fortune to sleep with the stars,

And to endure with the rain and the wind.

Grant me to love my life with zeal
And what besides thereto pertains;
Yet humbly I seek to be delivered
Of grovelling pathos and humiliation.

Since to my enemies, and them
That fawn upon my enemies,
I have my righteous hate in store,

E'en when the fearsome sun has stamped
Into my sockets his sunflower brand,
And I'm suddenly butchered like a beast,

What grudge and grievance should I bear
To you, O mighty sun of my life?

Yu Chi-Whan

Head

Here in December in the land of northernmost Manchuria,
Unblest by snow, and slashed by the dry ripping wind of the
    Amur,
Here at the cross-roads of a small stripped citadel town,
Are exposed high on stakes twin heads of whilom bandits;
Their dark purple faces shrivelled up like withered children,
And their half-open eyes staring into the distant polar circuit
Of hills and rivers beneath the sunset shimmer of the bladed sky.
Know you now in death the taste of the Judgment of Law?
It is not that death is one of the four evils
But that the preservation of peace renders at times
Human life as cheap as a chicken or a cur.
Your life might well have proved an instant threat of my death,
So that to rule out force by means of force has ever been
The sanction of blood from times primeval.
Now as I pace along this wind-swept thoroughfare,
I am resolved afresh of the dogged ferocity of life.
You who housed your uncontrollable souls of treachery,
Close your eyes in peace! May merciful heaven
Cover this landscape of waste thoughts with deep, deep snow!

Yu Chi-Whan
[183]

Mountain Lodge

Beside the closed bamboo gate
The blossom petals are trembling.

The very sound of water soaks
Into this cloud-encircled lodge.

Drenched in the welcome shower
The iris blades look fresh and cold.

A honey-bee drones past
The sun-bathed paper screen.

The rocks squat apart
Immovable and still,

And look proud beneath
Their green coat of moss.

In the soft vibration
Of a faint whirlwind,

The bracken sprouts
Roll up their fists.

Cho Ji-Hoon

[184]

Shedding of the Petals

What if the petals be shed,
Should the breeze be blamed?

The stars hung beyond the bamboo-screen
Are put out one by one.

The distant hills loom nearer
After the Philomel's song.

Should the candle be blown
Now the petals are falling in flakes?

The shadows of the petals falling
Are dimly cast upon the lawn,

And the white paper-screen
Is faintly flushed.

Lest the frail mind
Of him who lives in refuge

Be revealed to the vulgar,
I have some natural fears.

These petals that are shed in the dawn
Prompt some listless tears.

Cho Ji-Hoon

3610